Avocado Cookbook

Easy and Delicious Avocado Recipes Everyone Will Love

By
BookSumo Press
All rights reserved

Published by
http://www.booksumo.com

ENJOY THE RECIPES?

KEEP ON COOKING WITH 6 MORE FREE COOKBOOKS!

Visit our website and simply enter your email address to join the club and receive your 6 cookbooks.

http://booksumo.com/magnet

https://www.instagram.com/booksumopress/

https://www.facebook.com/booksumo/

LEGAL NOTES

All Rights Reserved. No Part Of This Book May Be Reproduced Or Transmitted In Any Form Or By Any Means. Photocopying, Posting Online, And / Or Digital Copying Is Strictly Prohibited Unless Written Permission Is Granted By The Book's Publishing Company. Limited Use Of The Book's Text Is Permitted For Use In Reviews Written For The Public.

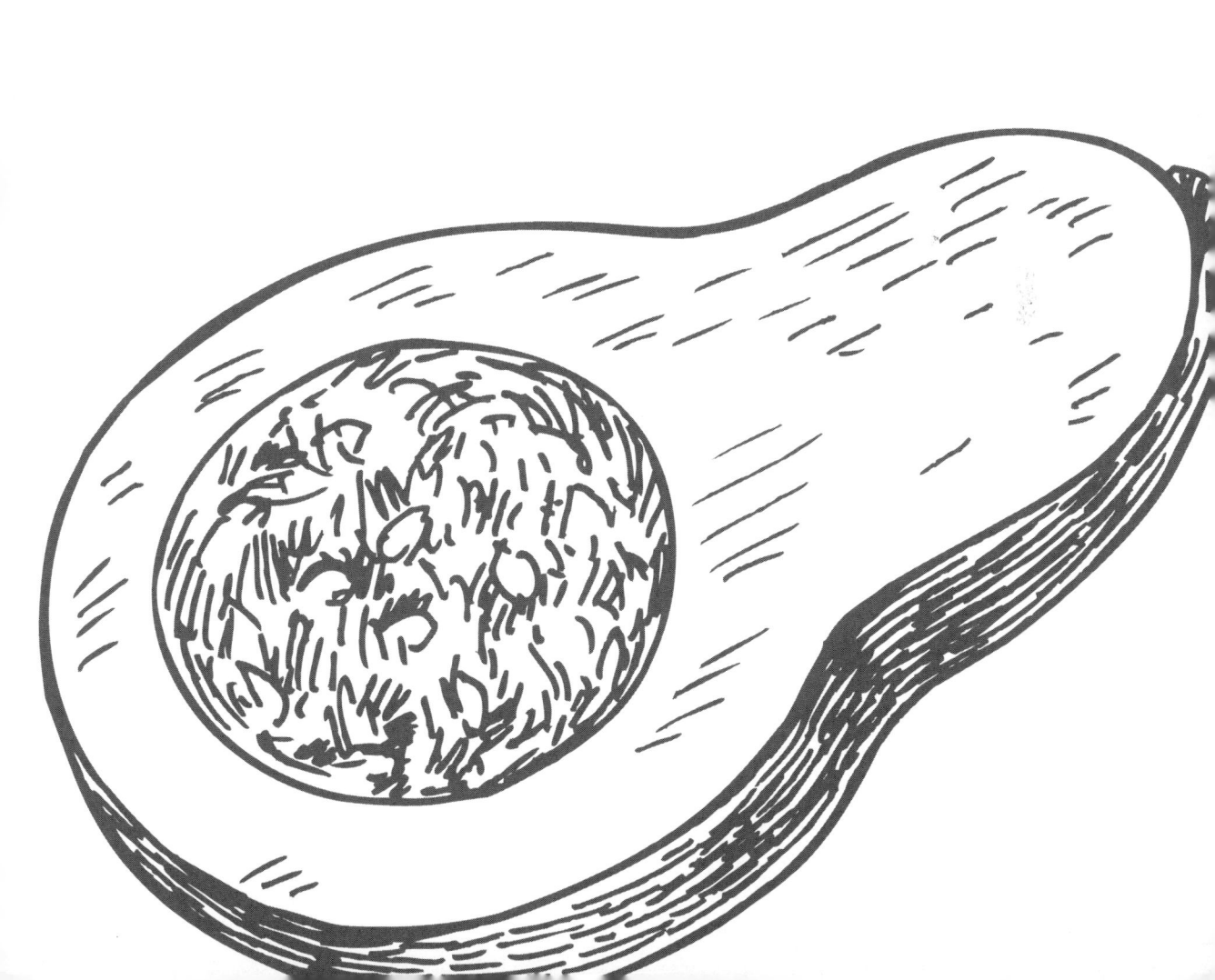

Table of Contents

Fresno Topped Cheddar Sandwiches 9

Sonoma BLT Wraps 10

Waco Ranch Wraps 11

Houston Club Wrap 12

Ventura Wraps 13

Chipotle Corn Wraps 14

Baja Wraps 15

Cheddar Salsa Wraps 16

Redmond Veggie Wraps 17

Dijon Genoa Wraps 18

Pesto Tilapia Lettuce Wraps 19

Chipotle Bean Wraps 20

Napa Valley Wraps 21

Peruvian Salad Dressing 22

Grilled Halibut Tacos 23

Tomato and Avocado Soup 24

Creamy Avocado Stew 25

Deviled Eggs California 26

Hot Mahi Mahi 27

California Topped Tofu 28

California Creole Salmon 29

Queen Rancho Soup 30

Chicken Soup Spicy Mexican Style 32

Avocado Milkshakes in the Philippines 33

Spiced Kale Ceviche 34

Ceviche Cups 35

Louisiana Ceviche 36

West Indian Ceviche 37

Sunday's Ceviche 38

Peruvian Salad Dressing 39

Avocado Papaya Salsa 40

Seattle Quinoa Bowls 41

Seattle Couscous Salad 42

Baja Avocados 43

California Salad 44

Los Angeles Lunch 45

Quinoa Cucumber Salad 46

October Avocado Salad 47

Shrimp and Avocado Picnic Salad 48

Milanese Greek Style Salad 49

Fresh Dijon Garden Salad 50

Alternative Fruit Salad 51

Southern Honey and Dijon Collard Green Salad 52

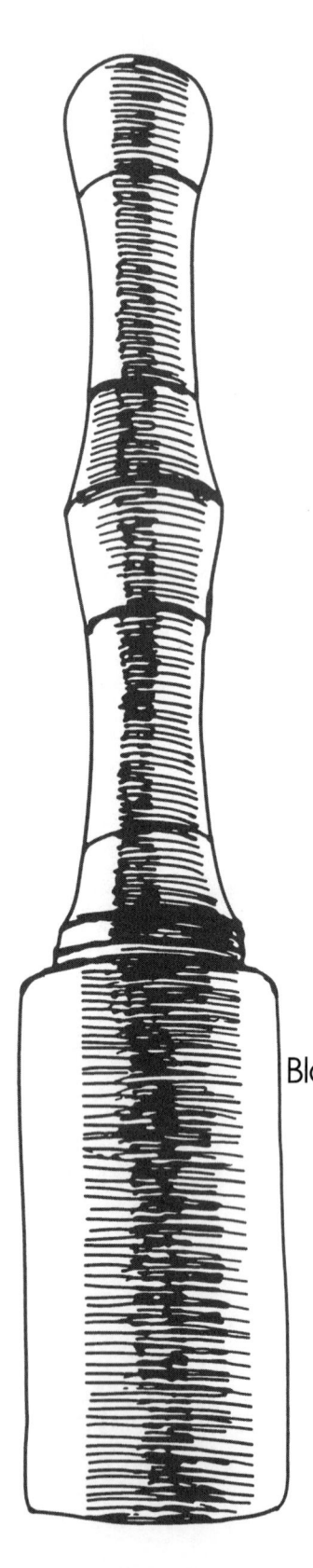

A Skinny Dinner 53

Alfalfa and Lentil Lunchbox 54

Simply Guacamole and Lime 55

Cookout Guacamole 56

Tis' the Season for Guacamole 57

San Miguel Inspired Guacamole 58

Peach and Grape Guacamole 59

Vegetarian Dream Guacamole 60

Macho Mayo Guacamole 61

3-Ingredient Guacamole 62

Bell Pepper Medley Guacamole 63

I ♥ Guacamole 64

Coarse Garlic Guacamole 65

Fajita Guacamole 66

Backroad Guacamole 67

Black & Yellow Guacamole with Corn 68

Honolulu County Guacamole 69

Sweet Smoked Guacamole 70

Sesame Thai Guacamole 71

Guacamole Dream 72

New-Age Guacamole 73

Guacamole for August 74

Tropical Guacamole 75

2-Pepper Guacamole 76

Kiwi Guacamole 77

Annabelle's Guacamole 78

Mediterranean Guacamole 79

California x Florida Popsicles 80

California Paletas 81

Avocado Arepas 82

Southwest Avocado Blend 83

Florida Avocado Lunch Box 84

Red Avocado Salsa 85

Spicy Green Hummus 86

Salad Cubana 87

Latin Bruschetta 88

Burgers Santa Domingo 89

Chicken Cutlets Chimichurri 90

Sonoma Black Bean Tacos 92

Topped Seafood Tacos 94

American Shrimp Flatbreads 95

Ceviche Cups 96

West Indian Ceviche 97

Naked Ceviche 98

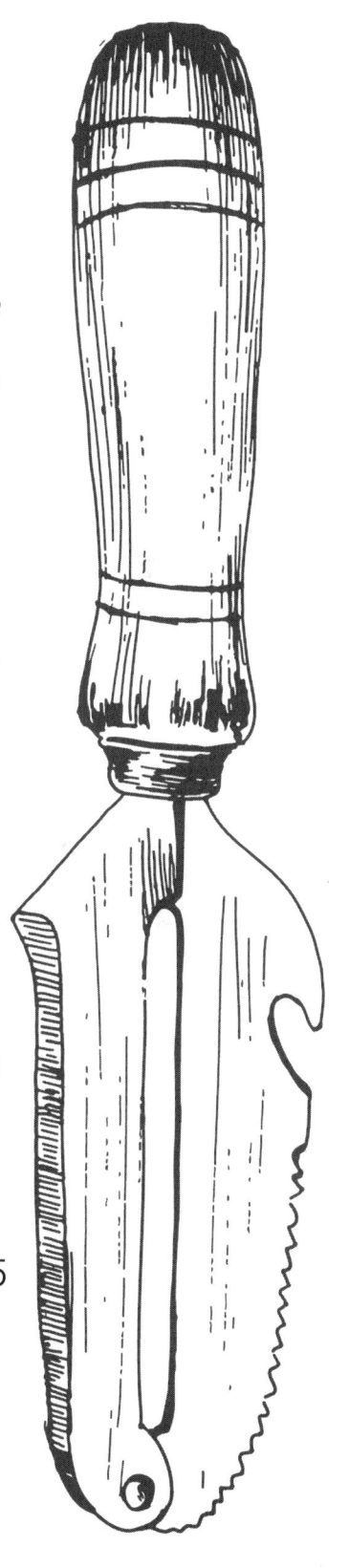

Bar Harbor Ceviche 99

Crunchy Crab Ceviche 100

Ceviche Tilapia 101

Ceviche Bowls 102

Sonoma Fruit Salad 103

Ground Turkey Tacos 104

Avocado & Tomato Dip 105

Fresno Topped Cheddar Sandwiches

Prep Time: 10 mins
Total Time: 15 mins

Servings per Recipe: 4
Calories   362.5
Fat   22.5g
Cholesterol   32.1mg
Sodium   468.8mg
Carbohydrates   29.1g
Protein   12.6g

Ingredients

4 whole wheat sandwich rounds
1 mashed avocado
1/2 C. chopped tomato
1/2 C. chopped red onion
2 tbsp ranch dressing
1 C. shredded cheddar cheese
salt and pepper

Directions

1. Set the broiler of your oven.
2. In a bowl, add the tomato, avocado and onion and mix well.
3. In the bottom of a baking sheet, arrange the sandwich rounds.
4. Place the avocado mixture onto each sandwich round evenly, followed by the dressing, cheese.
5. Sprinkle with the salt and pepper and cook under the broiler for about 5 minutes.
6. Enjoy hot.

SONOMA
BLT Wraps (Bacon Lettuce and Tomato)

Prep Time: 15 mins
Total Time: 25 mins

Servings per Recipe: 2
Calories 74.9
Fat 5.0g
Cholesterol 13.5mg
Sodium 290.1mg
Carbohydrates 3.1g
Protein 4.5g

Ingredients

2 slices cooked turkey bacon
1 medium tomatoes, sliced
1 green onion, sliced
1 tbsp shredded cheddar cheese
1 tsp sour cream
nice crispy lettuce
1 dash salt
1 dash pepper
avocado, sliced
1 dash Tabasco sauce

Directions

1. Place a pan over medium heat. Cook in it the bacon until it becomes crisp. Drain it.
2. Heat the tortillas in a pan for 10 to 15 sec on each side. Place them on serving plates.
3. Coat the upper side of the tortillas with sour cream, top it with cheese, lettuce, tomato, bacon, green onion, and avocado.
4. Season them with a pinch of salt and pepper. Wrap your tortillas carefully and slice them in half.
5. Serve your wraps with extra toppings of your choice.
6. Enjoy.

Waco Ranch Wraps

Prep Time: 15 mins
Total Time: 15 mins

Servings per Recipe: 4
Calories   1106.8
Fat   90.5g
Cholesterol   170.4mg
Sodium   1674.7mg
Carbohydrates   36.5g
Protein   39.6g

Ingredients

- 1 C. ranch dressing
- 4 flour tortillas, warmed
- 10 oz. cheese slices, your preference
- 2 tomatoes, sliced
- 1 (8 oz.) cream cheese, softened
- 10 oz. turkey breast, slices
- 2 avocados, sliced
- alfalfa sprout

Directions

1. Get a mixing bowl: Beat in it the cream cheese with ranch dressing until they become creamy.
2. Spoon the mixture into the tortillas and spread them into an even layer.
3. Top them with turkey, cheese, avocados, tomatoes, and sprouts. Roll the tortillas tightly then serve them.
4. Enjoy.

HOUSTON
Club Wrap

Prep Time: 5 mins
Total Time: 5 mins

Servings per Recipe: 1
Calories   8.0
Fat   0.0g
Cholesterol   0.0mg
Sodium   5.8mg
Carbohydrates   1.6g
Protein   0.4g

Ingredients

1 leaf red leaf lettuce
1 slice turkey breast
1 slice turkey ham, optional
1 slice tomatoes
1 slice avocado, mashed
1 tsp lime juice

1 leaf arugula
1 tbsp sugar-free ranch dressing

Directions

1. Get a mixing bowl: Mix in it the avocado with lime juice and a pinch of salt to make the salsa.
2. Lay a lettuce leaf on a cutting board. Top it with turkey, ham, tomato, avocado salsa, and arugula.
3. Wrap it around the filling tightly and press into it a toothpick to secure it.
4. Serve you wrap right away.
5. Enjoy.

Ventura Wraps

Prep Time: 30 mins
Total Time: 30 mins

Servings per Recipe: 4
Calories   693.8
Fat   49.1g
Cholesterol   75.0mg
Sodium   886.0mg
Carbohydrates   54.3g
Protein   14.4g

Ingredients

1 (8 oz.) packages cream cheese, softened
1/2 C. sour cream
1 (4 oz.) cans chopped green chilies, drained
1 tbsp taco seasoning
4 (10 inches) flour tortillas, warmed

2 medium ripe avocados, peeled and sliced
2 plum tomatoes, sliced
5 green onions, sliced
1 (4 oz.) cans sliced ripe olives, drained

Directions

1. Get a mixing bowl: Whisk in it the cream cheese, sour cream, chilies and taco seasoning until they become smooth.
2. Place the tortillas on a serving plate. Pour 1/4 C. of cream over each tortilla.
3. Arrange over them the avocado with tomato, onion, and olives. Fold your tortillas then serve them.
4. Enjoy.

CHIPOTLE
Corn Wraps

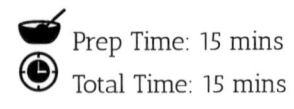

🥣 Prep Time: 15 mins
🕒 Total Time: 15 mins

Servings per Recipe: 2
Calories   433.3
Fat   28.7g
Cholesterol   61.8mg
Sodium   346.0mg
Carbohydrates   26.3g
Protein   20.9g

Ingredients

2 (12 inches) whole wheat tortillas, any flavor
1 1/2 tbsp cream cheese
1 tsp chipotle chile in adobo
4 leaves lettuce
4 slices Monterey jack pepper cheese
4 slices tomatoes
1/2 avocado, sliced

4 slices red onions
1/2 C. jicama, sliced into matchsticks
1/4 C. sweet corn, defrosted
1/2 C. cooked black beans, drained and rinsed

Directions

1. Place the tortillas on baking sheet. Top them with cream cheese, lettuce, jack cheese, tomato, avocado, onion, and jicama.
2. Top them with corn, bean, a pinch of salt and pepper. Wrap your tortillas tightly then serve them.
3. Enjoy.

Baja Wraps

Prep Time: 15 mins
Total Time: 25 mins

Servings per Recipe: 4
Calories   233.8
Fat   1.2g
Cholesterol   0.0mg
Sodium   6.8mg
Carbohydrates   50.9g
Protein   9.1g

Ingredients

- 1 red bell pepper, seeded, chopped
- 1 green bell pepper, seeded, chopped
- 1 onion, peeled, sliced
- 1 (15 oz.) cans black beans, low sodium, drained, rinsed
- 2 mangoes, peeled, pitted, chopped
- 1 lime, juice
- 1/2 C. fresh cilantro, chopped
- 1 avocado, peeled, pitted, diced
- 4 (10 inches) fat-free tortillas

Directions

1. Place a large skillet over medium heat. Coat it with a cooking spray.
2. Cook in it the bell peppers with onion for 6 min. Stir in the beans and cook them for extra 6 min.
3. Get a mixing bowl: Stir in it the mangoes, lime juice, and cilantro to make the salsa.
4. Spoon the bell pepper and beans mixture into the tortillas. Top them with the mango salsa and roll them tightly.
5. Slice your wraps in half then serve them.
6. Enjoy.

CHEDDAR
Salsa Wraps

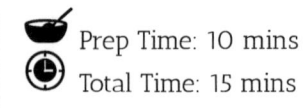

Prep Time: 10 mins
Total Time: 15 mins

Servings per Recipe: 4
Calories 467.0
Fat 22.1g
Cholesterol 77.8mg
Sodium 722.4mg
Carbohydrates 40.4g
Protein 25.6g

Ingredients

2 avocados, pitted peeled and sliced
2 (16 oz.) cans black beans, drained and rinsed
2 large tomatoes, diced
4 oz. salsa
1/2 tsp cumin
1/4 C. cilantro

1/4 C. cheddar cheese, shredded
4 oz. spinach
4 tortillas

Directions

1. Get a mixing bowl: Stir in it the avocado, beans, tomato, salsa, cumin, and cilantro.
2. Spoon the mixture into the tortillas. Arrange over them the spinach and cheese.
3. Fold your tortillas burrito style then serve them.
4. Enjoy.

Redmond Veggie Wraps

🥣 Prep Time: 15 mins
🕐 Total Time: 23 mins

Servings per Recipe: 1
Calories   335.5
Fat   11.8g
Cholesterol   0.3mg
Sodium   89.8mg
Carbohydrates   50.5g
Protein   16.4g

Ingredients

- 24 asparagus spears
- 1 ripe avocado, pitted and peeled
- 1 tbsp lime juice
- 1 garlic clove, minced
- 1 1/2 C. cooked long-grain brown rice, cold
- 3 tbsp plain nonfat yogurt
- 3 (10 inches) whole wheat tortillas
- 1/3 C. cilantro leaf
- 2 tbsp chopped red onions

Directions

1. Place a large saucepan over high heat. Heat in it 2 inches of water.
2. Place over it a basket and cook in it the asparagus with a lid on for 7 to 9 min.
3. Once the time is up, place it in an ice bowl and drain it.
4. Get a mixing bowl: Mix in it the avocado, lime juice, and garlic to make the salsa.
5. Get a mixing bowl: Mix in it the rice with yogurt.
6. Place a large skillet over medium heat. Warm in it the tortillas for few seconds on each side.
7. Place the tortillas on serving plates. Top them with the avocado salsa followed by the yogurt mixture, asparagus, cilantro, and onion.
8. Fold your tortillas burrito style. Wrap them in a cling foil and place them in the fridge for 70 min.
9. Once the time is up, slice your wraps in half then serve them.
10. Enjoy.

DIJON
Genoa Wraps

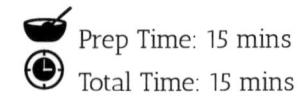

🥣 Prep Time: 15 mins
🕒 Total Time: 15 mins

Servings per Recipe: 1
Calories	1104.3
Fat	63.6g
Cholesterol	47.2mg
Sodium	7971.9mg
Carbohydrates	101.4g
Protein	44.8g

Ingredients

1 tbsp cider vinegar
salt
pepper
1/2 medium red onion, sliced
2 small firm avocados, cut in wedges
4 large flour tortillas
4 oz. baby spring greens

6 oz. Genoa salami, sliced and cut into strips
Spread
3 tbsp Dijon mustard
2 tbsp balsamic vinegar
1/4 C. mayonnaise

Directions

1. Get a mixing bowl: Whisk in it the mustard with vinegar, and mayo.
2. Spread the mixture all over the tortillas leaving the sides empty.
3. Top them with a layer of onion, avocados, salami and spring onions.
4. Season them with some salt. Roll the tortilla over the filling tightly then serve them.
5. Enjoy.

Pesto Tilapia Lettuce Wraps

Prep Time: 20 mins
Total Time: 40 mins

Servings per Recipe: 2
Calories   3041.5
Fat   284.2g
Cholesterol   177.5mg
Sodium   2460.3mg
Carbohydrates   84.1g
Protein   54.8g

Ingredients

2 - 3 tilapia fillets
1 avocado, sliced
16 oz. canola oil
1 head iceberg lettuce
Batter
1 tsp Old Bay Seasoning
1 tsp salt
1 tsp black pepper
1 tsp cayenne pepper
1/2 tsp garlic powder
3/4 C. wheat flour
3/4 C. panko breadcrumbs

1 egg
1/2-1 C. water
Pesto
1/2 C. roasted red pepper
1/4 C. Greek yogurt
2 garlic cloves
1/2 C. bunch basil
1/2 C. parmesan and pecorino cheese blend
1/2 tsp pepper
1/4 C. olive oil

Directions

1. To prepare the batter:
2. Get a mixing bowl:: Mix in it the all the batter ingredients.
3. Cut each fish fillet into 3 pieces. Dip them completely in the batter.
4. Place a large deep pan over medium heat. Heat in it 3 inches of oil.
5. Deep fry in it the fish pieces until they become golden brown. Drain them and place them on paper towels to dry.
6. Get a food processor: Place in it all the pepper pesto ingredients. Season them with a pinch of salt. Blend them smooth.
7. Overlap each 2 lettuce leaves on a serving plate. Top them with fried fish followed by avocado and pepper pesto.
8. Serve your open wraps immediately. Enjoy.

CHIPOTLE
Bean Wraps

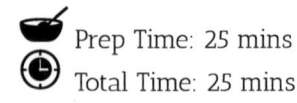

Prep Time: 25 mins
Total Time: 25 mins

Servings per Recipe: 4
Calories 399.8
Fat 14.3g
Cholesterol 0.0mg
Sodium 633.1mg
Carbohydrates 56.7g
Protein 13.8g

Ingredients

2 tbsp cider vinegar
1 tbsp canola oil
2 tsp chopped canned chipotle chilies in adobo
1/4 tsp salt
2 C. shredded red cabbage
1 medium carrot, shredded
1/4 C. chopped cilantro
1 (15 oz.) cans white beans, rinsed
1 ripe avocado
1/2 C. shredded sharp cheddar cheese
2 tbsp minced red onions
4 whole wheat tortillas

Directions

1. Get a mixing bowl: Mix in it the vinegar, oil, chipotle chile and salt.
2. Stir in the carrot with cabbage, and cilantro. place it aside.
3. Get a mixing bowl: Mix in it the avocado with beans until they become chunky.
4. Fold the cheese and onion into the mixture.
5. Warm the tortillas in the microwave for few seconds. Top them with a layer of avocado spread followed by cabbage salad.
6. Roll the tortillas over the filling tightly. Serve them immediately.
7. Enjoy.

Napa Valley Wraps

Prep Time: 15 mins
Total Time: 15 mins

Servings per Recipe: 4
Calories   416.7
Fat   9.5g
Cholesterol   0.0mg
Sodium   155.1mg
Carbohydrates   77.8g
Protein   25.0g

Ingredients

3 oranges peeled and sliced.
1/2 avocado
2 sprigs dill
1/2 head napa cabbage, sliced
2 tomatoes, sliced
12 romaine leaves

Directions

1. Get a food processor: Place in it 2 slices oranges with dill and avocado.
2. Blend them smooth to make the dressing.
3. Get a large mixing bowl: Chop the remaining orange and stir it with cabbage and orange dressing.
4. Spoon the mixture into romaine leaves. Garnish them with tomato slices then serve them.
5. Enjoy.

PERUVIAN Salad Dressing (Cilantro Based)

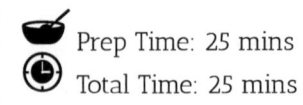

Prep Time: 25 mins
Total Time: 25 mins

Servings per Recipe: 12
Calories   42 kcal
Fat   4.1 g
Carbohydrates   1.6g
Protein   < 0.3 g
Cholesterol   < 0 mg
Sodium   2 mg

Ingredients

1/3 C. olive oil
1 clove garlic, minced
3/4 C. diced fresh cilantro
2 avocados, peeled, seeded and cubed
1 large cucumber, peeled, seeded and cut into chunks
1/4 C. lemon juice
salt and pepper to taste

Directions

1. Puree all the ingredients in a food processor for 1 min while pouring in the olive oil.
2. Once all the oil has been adding continue to puree the dressing for another 60 secs.
3. Add in some pepper and salt then pulse the dressing a few more times until it is smooth.
4. Enjoy chilled.

Grilled Halibut Tacos

Prep Time: 15 mins
Total Time: 25 mins

Servings per Recipe: 4
Calories   689.0
Fat   27.6g
Cholesterol   91.9mg
Sodium   1322.6mg
Carbohydrates   68.0g
Protein   46.0g

Ingredients

- 4 halibut steaks
- olive oil
- salt and pepper
- 1 lime, juiced
- 3 medium ripe Hass avocadoes, scooped
- 1 lemon, juiced
- 1/2 tsp cayenne pepper
- 1 C. plain yogurt
- 1 tsp salt
- 2 plum tomatoes, seeded and chopped
- 2 scallions, sliced
- 1 romaine lettuce hearts
- 12 flour tortillas

Directions

1. Before you do anything, preheat the grill and grease it.
2. Coat the halibut fillets with some olive oil. Sprinkle over them some salt and pepper.
3. Place the fish fillets on the grill and cook them for 4 to 6 min on each side. Drizzle over them the juice of 1 lime while they're cooking.
4. Get a food processor: Blend in it the avocado flesh, lemon juice, cayenne pepper, yogurt and salt.
5. Pour the mixture into a bowl. Fold into it the diced tomato and scallions to make the guacamole.
6. Heat the tortillas in a pan. Flake the fish and place divide it between the tortillas.
7. Top them with the guacamole followed by the shredded lettuce and your other favorite toppings.
8. Fold your tacos then serve them right away.
9. Enjoy.

TOMATO and Avocado Soup

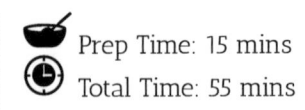

Prep Time: 15 mins
Total Time: 55 mins

Servings per Recipe: 12
Calories 315 kcal
Fat 16.2 g
Carbohydrates 37.2g
Protein 8.7 g
Cholesterol 12 mg
Sodium 1152 mg

Ingredients

- 2 tbsps vegetable oil
- 1 (1 lb) package frozen pepper and onion veggie mix
- 2 cloves garlic, diced
- 3 tbsps ground cumin
- 1 (28 oz.) can crushed tomatoes
- 3 (4 oz.) cans chopped green chili peppers, drained
- 4 (14 oz.) cans vegetable broth
- salt and pepper to taste
- 1 (11 oz.) can whole kernel corn
- 12 oz. tortilla chips
- 1 C. shredded Cheddar cheese
- 1 avocado, peeled, pitted and diced

Directions

1. Stir fry your onions and peppers for 2 mins in hot oil then add in the cumin and garlic. Continue frying the mix for 4 more mins until the veggies are soft.
2. Now combine in the chili peppers and tomatoes.
3. Stir the mix again and let the pepper cook for 30 secs before adding in some pepper, salt, and the broth.
4. Now get everything boiling, set the heat to low, and let the mix gently simmer for 35 mins.
5. Add in the corn to the mix and let the veggies cook for 7 mins.
6. When serving the soup top each individual serving with some tortilla chips, avocado, and cheese.
7. Enjoy.

Creamy Avocado Stew

Prep Time: 15 mins
Total Time: 55 mins

Servings per Recipe: 4
Calories	410 kcal
Fat	40.6 g
Carbohydrates	12.5g
Protein	3.9 g
Cholesterol	82 mg
Sodium	374 mg

Ingredients

- 2 avocado, peeled, pitted and diced
- 1 tbsp chopped shallots
- 1 tbsp olive oil
- 2 C. chicken stock
- 1 C. heavy cream
- salt and pepper to taste
- 1/4 tsp ground nutmeg
- 1 tomato, peeled, seeded and diced

Directions

1. Add your avocado to the bowl of a food processor and begin to puree it.
2. Begin to stir fry your shallots in olive oil until they are soft then shut the heat.
3. Get a bowl, combine: chicken stock, shallots, cream, and avocado.
4. Stir the mix until it is smooth then add in the nutmeg, some pepper and salt.
5. Place a covering of plastic on the bowl and put the mix in the fridge for 30 mins.
6. When serving the dish top the soup with your tomatoes.
7. Enjoy.

DEVILED EGGS
California

Prep Time: 10 mins
Total Time: 15 mins

Servings per Recipe: 12
Calories 66.2
Fat 5.1g
Cholesterol 93.2mg
Sodium 48.1mg
Carbohydrates 1.8g
Protein 3.5g

Ingredients

6 hard-boiled eggs, halved and yolks removed
1 avocado, mashed
2 tbsps. salsa

Topping
12 cilantro leaves

Directions

1. Place the mashed avocado and salsa in a bowl and combine well.
2. Insert the avocado mixture into each egg white.
3. Sprinkle with parsley or cilantro and serve.
4. Enjoy.

Hot Mahi Mahi

Prep Time: 15 mins
Total Time: 27 mins

Servings per Recipe: 6	
Calories	285.1
Fat	8.8 g
Cholesterol	165.4 mg
Sodium	592.5 mg
Carbohydrates	7.5 g
Protein	43.1 g

Ingredients

Salsa
- 1 ripe avocado, peeled and cubed
- 2 Roma tomatoes, diced
- 1 C. minced red onion
- 1 jalapeno pepper, minced
- 1/2 C. cilantro
- 1 lime, juice
- 1/2 tsp kosher salt

Mahi Mahi
- 3 lbs. mahi-mahi, cut into 6 pieces
- 1 tbsp extra virgin olive oil
- 1 lime, juice
- 1/2 tsp kosher salt

Directions

1. To prepare the salsa:
2. Get a mixing bowl: Stir in it all the salsa ingredients.
3. Chill it in the fridge until ready to serve.
4. To prepare the grilled mahi-mahi:
5. Get a mixing bowl: Whisk in it the olive oil, lime, salt, and pepper.
6. Add to it the fish strips and toss them to coat.
7. Cover them and chill them in the fridge for 25 to 35 min.
8. Before you do anything, preheat the grill and grease it.
9. Drain the fish strips from the marinade and grill them for 7 to 9 min on each side.
10. Serve your grilled fish with avocado salsa.
11. Enjoy.

CALIFORNIA
Topped Tofu

Prep Time: 3 hrs
Total Time: 3 hrs 20 mins

Servings per Recipe: 4
Calories 207.9
Fat 8.9 g
Cholesterol 0.0 mg
Sodium 205.5 mg
Carbohydrates 32.7 g
Protein 4.7 g

Ingredients

- 2 packages firm tofu, drained
- 2 Texas starred grapefruits
- 3 navel oranges
- 4 tsp olive oil
- 3/4 tsp cayenne pepper
- 1/4 tsp salt, divided
- 1/2 red bell pepper, seeded and minced
- 1/4 red onion, minced
- 2 tbsp fresh cilantro, minced and packed
- 1 bag Florentine Baby Spinach, washed and dried
- 1/2 avocado, ripe but firm, diced

Directions

1. To prepare the tofu:
2. Slice the tofu block then cut each slice into 2 pieces making two triangles. Get a mixing bowl: Whisk in it the juice of half grapefruit with the juice of half an orange, and 1 tbsp of oil.
3. Pat the tofu slices dry then arrange them in a roasting dish.
4. Pour over them the juice mixture. Layover it a plastic wrap to cover it. Let it sit overnight in the fridge.
5. To prepare the salsa:
6. Peel and cut the remaining grapefruits and oranges into segments.
7. Get a mixing bowl: Stir in it the fruit segments with bell pepper, red onion, cilantro and a pinch of salt. Place it in the fridge until ready to serve.
8. Place a grilling pan over medium heat. Heat in it 1 tsp of olive oil. Stir in it the tofu with its marinade. Let them cook for 3 to 4 min on each side. Once the time is up, drain them and transfer them to a serving plate.
9. Stir the spinach into the same pan and cook them for 2 min. Transfer the spinach into serving plates followed by tofu slices and fruit salsa. Enjoy.

California
Creole Salmon

Prep Time: 15 mins
Total Time: 25 mins

Servings per Recipe: 4
Calories   539.5
Fat   32.9 g
Cholesterol   78.2 mg
Sodium   141.3 mg
Carbohydrates   25.7 g
Protein   39.5 g

Ingredients

3/4 C. frozen corn
2 tomatoes, cored and chopped
2 avocados, halved, pitted & diced
1/2 red onion, chopped
2 tbsp parsley, chopped
3 tbsp olive oil
2 tbsp lemon juice
kosher salt and ground pepper

4 (6 oz.) salmon, filets
1/2 tsp creole seasoning, see appendix

Directions

1. Before you do anything, preheat the grill and grease it.
2. Get a large mixing bowl: Mix in it the corn, tomatoes, avocados, onion, parsley, olive oil and lemon juice.
3. Stir in a pinch of creole seasoning, a pinch of salt and pepper.
4. Place the tomato relish in the fridge until ready to serve.
5. Coat the salmon steaks with olive oil. Season them with a pinch of creole seasoning.
6. Grill them for 4 to 5 min on each side.
7. Serve your grilled salmon right away with tomato relish.
8. Enjoy.

QUEEN RANCHO
Soup

Prep Time: 1 hr
Total Time: 1 hr

Servings per Recipe: 6
Calories 336.2
Fat 19.8g
Cholesterol 12.5mg
Sodium 1090.4mg
Carbohydrates 31.4g
Protein 14.0g

Ingredients

4 corn tortillas
3 tbsp salad oil
1 onion, peeled and finely chopped
1 dried bay leaf
1/2 tsp dried oregano
1/2 tsp black peppercorns
1/2 tsp hot chili flakes
8 C. fat-skimmed chicken broth
1 avocado
1 lime
3/4 C. shredded Monterey jack cheese
salt and pepper

salsa fresca
1 lb tomatoes
1 fresh jalapeno
1/4 C. finely chopped onion
1/4 C. chopped fresh cilantro
3 tbsp lime juice
salt and pepper

Directions

1. Cut the tortillas into 1-inch-wide strips. In a 5-6-quart pan, heat the oil on high heat and cook the tortilla strips for about 2-3 minutes, stirring occasionally.
2. Transfer the tortilla strips onto the paper towels lined plate to drain. In the same pan, add the onion and garlic on medium-high heat and sauté for about 3-4 minutes.
3. Stir in the bay leaf, oregano, peppercorns, chili flakes and broth and bring to a boil on high heat.
4. Cook for about 20-25 minutes. Meanwhile for the salsa, rinse and core the tomatoes. Cut each tomato into 1/4-inch pieces and transfer into a bowl with their juices.
5. Rinse the jalapeño pepper and remove the stems and seeds. Then, cut out the veins and chop it finely.
6. In the bowl of the tomatoes, add the jalapeño pepper, onion, cilantro, and 3 tbsp of the lime juice, salt and pepper and gently, stir to combine.

7. In a blender, add half of the salsa and pulse till puréed roughly.
8. Add the puréed salsa into hot soup with the salt and pepper and stir to combine.
9. Pit, peel and thinly slice the avocado.
10. Cut the lime into thin slices crosswise and discard the ends.
11. In wide soup bowls, divide the tortilla strips, remaining salsa, avocado slices, lime slices, and jack cheese.
12. Top with the soup and serve.

CHICKEN SOUP
Spicy Mexican Style

Prep Time: 20 mins
Total Time: 40 mins

Servings per Recipe: 8
Calories	377 kcal
Fat	19.1 g
Carbohydrates	30.9 g
Protein	23.1 g
Cholesterol	46 mg
Sodium	943 mg

Ingredients

1 onion, chopped
3 cloves garlic, minced
1 tbsp olive oil
2 tsp chili powder
1 tsp dried oregano
1 (28 oz.) can crushed tomatoes
1 (10.5 oz.) can condensed chicken broth
1 1/4 C. water
1 C. whole corn kernels, cooked
1 C. white hominy
1 (4 oz.) can chopped green chili peppers
1 (15 oz.) can black beans, rinsed and drained
1/4 C. chopped fresh cilantro
2 boneless chicken breast halves, cooked and cut into bite-sized pieces
Crushed tortilla chips
Sliced avocado
Shredded Monterey Jack cheese
Chopped green onions

Directions

1. In a large pan, heat the oil on medium heat and sauté the onion and garlic till soft.
2. Stir in the chili powder, oregano, tomatoes, broth and water and bring to a boil.
3. Simmer for about 5-10 minutes.
4. Stir in the corn, hominy, chilis, beans, cilantro, and chicken and simmer for about 10 minutes.
5. Transfer the soup into serving bowls and serve with a topping of the crushed tortilla chips, avocado slices, cheese and chopped green onion.

Avocado Milkshakes in the Philippines

Prep Time: 5 mins
Total Time: 5 mins

Servings per Recipe: 6
Calories   336 kcal
Carbohydrates   37.6 g
Cholesterol   18 mg
Fat   19.1 g
Protein   7.8 g
Sodium   84 mg

Ingredients

1 avocado - peeled, pitted, and cubed
5 cubes ice
3 tbsps white sugar
1 1/3 C. milk

1 tsp fresh lemon or lime juice
1 scoop vanilla ice cream

Directions

1. Blend all the ingredients mentioned above in a blender until required smoothness is achieved.
2. Serve.

SPICED
Kale Ceviche

Prep Time: 10 mins
Total Time: 10 mins

Servings per Recipe: 6
Calories 117.8
Fat 6.3g
Cholesterol 0.0mg
Sodium 121.6mg
Carbohydrates 15.7g
Protein 2.6g

Ingredients

1 bunch kale, leaves
1 large avocado, peeled
1 tbsp lemon juice
1/4 tsp salt
1/2 tsp crushed red pepper flakes
1/2 red bell pepper
1 small carrot, grated
1/2 purple onion, chopped
1 1/2 C. mandarin orange segments

Directions

1. Get a mixing bowl: Toss in it the kale with avocado, lemon juice, salt and red pepper flakes.
2. Mix them well with your hands until they avocado become mashed and smooth.
3. Add the rest of the ingredients. Toss them to coat.
4. Chill your ceviche in the fridge for 35 min then serve it.
5. Enjoy.

Ceviche Cups

Prep Time: 10 mins
Total Time: 10 mins

Servings per Recipe: 4
Calories   278.8
Fat   15.1g
Cholesterol   37.4mg
Sodium   346.6mg
Carbohydrates   15.1g
Protein   23.6g

Ingredients

- 2 (6 oz.) cans albacore tuna in water, drained
- 1/2 C. sweet onion, diced
- 1 large tomatoes, seeded and diced
- 1 small cucumber, peeled and diced
- 1/4 C. cilantro,
- 1 - 2 serrano chili, diced
- 2 - 3 limes, juice
- 1 tbsp olive oil
- salt
- pepper
- 1 large avocado, diced
- 8 tostadas

Directions

1. Get a mixing bowl: Stir in it the tuna, onion, tomato, cucumber, and cilantro.
2. Pour over them the lime juice, olive oil, salt, and pepper. Toss them to coat.
3. Stir in the serrano chilies, followed by avocado.
4. Spoon your ceviche into tostadas then serve them right away.
5. Enjoy.

LOUISIANA
Ceviche

Prep Time: 1 hr
Total Time: 5 hr

Servings per Recipe: 12
Calories	207.6
Fat	14.0g
Cholesterol	41.5mg
Sodium	467.1mg
Carbohydrates	9.3g
Protein	12.8g

Ingredients

- 1 lb. catfish fillet, cut into pieces
- 1 tsp grated lemon zest
- 1/2 C. lemon juice
- 1 tsp grated lime zest
- 1/2 C. lime juice
- 2 tbsp extra-virgin olive oil
- 1 C. seeded diced ripe tomatoes
- 1/2 C. diced red onion
- 2 garlic cloves, sliced
- 2 tbsp cilantro leaves
- 1 tbsp oregano leaves
- 1 jalapeno pepper, seeded, deveined, and minced
- 1 tsp salt
- 1/2 tsp sugar
- 1 avocado, pitted, peeled, and diced

Directions

1. Get a Ziploc bag; stir in it the fish with lemon and lime zest and juices.
2. Seal the bag and shake it to coat. Place it in the fridge for 5 h to 18 h.
3. Once the time is up, drain the fish and transfer it to a mixing bowl.
4. Add to it the rest of the ingredients and toss them to coat. Serve it with some crackers.
5. Enjoy.

West Indian Ceviche

🥣 Prep Time: 40 mins
🕐 Total Time: 42 mins

Servings per Recipe: 4
Calories   470.4
Fat   13.0g
Cholesterol   265.0mg
Sodium   1131.5mg
Carbohydrates   61.3g
Protein   42.5g

Ingredients

- 1/2 lb. salmon, cubed
- 1 lb. of shell-less shrimp
- 1 big mango, peeled and diced
- 1/2 red onion, diced
- 4 small tomatoes, peeled and diced
- 1 chile serrano pepper, chopped
- cilantro, to desire
- 1 avocado, diced
- 20 limes, juice

Directions

1. Get a mixing bowl: Stir in it the shrimp and salmon with lime juice. Season them with a pinch of salt.
2. Cover the bowl and place it in the fridge for 2 h 30 min.
3. Once the time is up, drain the shrimp and salmon. Transfer them to another mixing bowl.
4. Add the remaining ingredients and toss them to coat.
5. Spoon your ceviche into serving glasses and serve them.
6. Enjoy.

SUNDAY'S
Ceviche

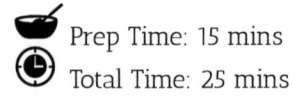

Prep Time: 15 mins
Total Time: 25 mins

Servings per Recipe: 4
Calories 236.9
Fat 10.8g
Cholesterol 56.7mg
Sodium 344.3mg
Carbohydrates 13.4g
Protein 25.0g

Ingredients

1 lb. tilapia fillet, cut into pieces
1 - 2 jalapeno pepper, minced
1/2 C. lime juice
1/2 C. fresh cilantro, chopped and divided
1 tsp fresh oregano, chopped
1/4 tsp salt
1 large green bell pepper, halved crosswise and sliced

1 large tomatoes, chopped
1/2 C. white onion, sliced
1/4 C. green olives, quartered
1 avocado, chopped

Directions

1. Place a pan over high heat. Place in it the fish and cover it with water. Cook it until it starts boiling.
2. Turn off the heat and cover the pan. Let the fish sit for 6 min.
3. Get a mixing bowl: Stir in it the fish after draining it with bell pepper, tomato, onion, and olives.
4. Cover the bowl and chill it in the fridge for 25 min.
5. Once the time is up, add the rest of the avocado and cilantro.
6. Adjust the seasoning of your ceviche then serve it.
7. Enjoy.

Peruvian Salad Dressing (Cilantro Based)

Prep Time: 25 mins
Total Time: 25 mins

Servings per Recipe: 32
Calories   42 kcal
Fat   4.1 g
Carbohydrates   1.6 g
Protein   < 0.3 g
Cholesterol   < 0 mg
Sodium   2 mg

Ingredients

- 1/3 C. olive oil
- 1 clove garlic, minced
- 3/4 C. diced fresh cilantro
- 2 avocados, peeled, seeded and cubed
- 1 large cucumber, peeled, seeded and cut into chunks
- 1/4 C. lemon juice
- salt and pepper to taste

Directions

1. Puree all the ingredients in a food processor for 1 min while pouring in the olive oil.
2. Once all the oil has been adding continue to puree the dressing for another 60 secs.
3. Add in some pepper and salt then pulse the dressing a few more times until it is smooth.
4. Enjoy chilled.

AVOCADO
Papaya Salsa

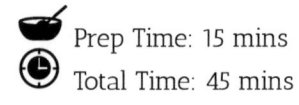

Prep Time: 15 mins
Total Time: 45 mins

Servings per Recipe: 8
Calories 77 kcal
Fat 3.9 g
Carbohydrates 11g
Protein 1.1 g
Cholesterol 0 mg
Sodium 5 mg

Ingredients

1 mango - peeled, seeded and diced
1 papaya - peeled, seeded and diced
1 large red bell pepper, seeded and diced
1 avocado - peeled, pitted and diced
1/2 sweet onion, peeled and diced
2 tbsp chopped fresh cilantro
2 tbsp balsamic vinegar
salt and pepper to taste

Directions

1. In a bowl, mix together the mango, papaya, red bell pepper, avocado, sweet onion, cilantro, balsamic vinegar, salt and pepper.
2. Refrigerate, covered to chill for at least 30 minutes before serving.

Seattle Quinoa Bowls

Prep Time: 10 mins
Total Time: 25 mins

Servings per Recipe: 6
Calories   210.2
Fat   11.8g
Cholesterol   0.0mg
Sodium   58.1mg
Carbohydrates   22.6g
Protein   5.1g

Ingredients

Vinaigrette
2 tbsp extra virgin olive oil
2 tbsp lemon juice
2 tbsp seasoned rice vinegar
1 garlic clove, minced
sea salt & ground black pepper
Salad
1 C. quinoa, rinsed and drained
2 C. water
2 C. chopped spinach

1 C. roasted chicken, shredded
1 medium avocado, peeled and chopped
1/4 C. sliced green onion
1/4 C. basil, chopped
8 kalamata olives, pitted and quartered
Optional Garnishes
steamed green beans
hard boiled eggs, sliced in half, or diced

Directions

1. For the vinaigrette: in a bowl, add all the ingredients and beat until well combined.
2. In a pan of the boiling water, cook the quinoa for about 15 minutes.
3. Remove from the heat and stir in vinaigrette and remaining ingredients and optional garnishes.
4. Enjoy.

SEATTLE
Couscous Salad

Prep Time: 30 mins
Total Time: 30 mins

Servings per Recipe: 6
Calories   317.0
Fat   6.5g
Cholesterol   9.8mg
Sodium   222.9mg
Carbohydrates   53.4g
Protein   12.3g

Ingredients

1 1/2 C. couscous
1 1/2 C. vegetable stock
1/4 tsp cumin
1/4 tsp coriander
1/4 tsp turmeric
1/4 tsp black pepper
1/4 tsp oregano
1/4 C. cilantro, chopped
3 tomatoes, seeded and diced
3 garlic cloves, minced
1/4 red onion, diced
1 carrot, grated

1/2 C. frozen corn, thawed
1/2 C. frozen peas, thawed
1/2 avocado, diced
1/2 C. canned chick-peas, drained and rinsed
1/2 C. canned black beans, drained and rinsed
1/2 C. cheddar cheese, grated

Directions

1. Place a pot over medium heat. Heat in it the stock until it starts boiling. Add the couscous and put on the lid.
2. Let it sit for 10 min. Fluff it with a fork.
3. Get a mixing bowl: Toss in it the remaining ingredients.
4. Add the couscous and stir them well. Adjust the seasoning of your salad then serve it.
5. Enjoy.

Baja Avocados

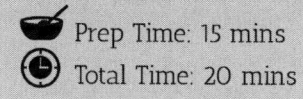

Prep Time: 15 mins
Total Time: 20 mins

Servings per Recipe: 8
Calories   204.0
Fat   14.5 g
Cholesterol   0.0 mg
Sodium   19.9 mg
Carbohydrates   18.0 g
Protein   4.4 g

Ingredients

- 4 Hass avocados, halved and pitted
- 2 tbsp lemon juice
- 2 tbsp extra virgin olive oil
- Salsa
- 8 oz. gold & white corn, strained
- 1/2 tbsp ground cumin
- 8 oz. black beans, strained
- 1/2 tbsp chili powder
- 1 medium tomatoes, diced
- 1 tbsp cilantro, chopped
- 1/2 medium white onion, diced
- salt & pepper
- corn chips

Directions

1. Set your grill for medium-high heat and grease the grill grate.
2. Coat each avocado half with the lemon juice and then with the oil evenly.
3. Arrange each avocado half onto the grill, skin side down and cook for about 4 minutes, flipping once half way through.
4. Meanwhile, for the salsa: in a bowl, add all the ingredients and mix well.
5. Enjoy the avocados warm with a topping of the salsa.

CALIFORNIA
Salad

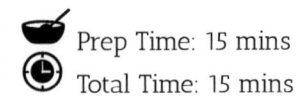

Prep Time: 15 mins
Total Time: 15 mins

Servings per Recipe: 4
Calories   257 kcal
Fat   23.2 g
Carbohydrates   10g
Protein   6.2 g
Cholesterol   4 mg
Sodium   381 mg

Ingredients

4 C. young arugula leaves, rinsed and dried
1 C. cherry tomatoes, halved
1/4 C. pine nuts
2 tbsp olive oil
1 tbsp rice vinegar
salt to taste
freshly ground black pepper to taste
1/4 C. grated Parmesan cheese
1 large avocado - peeled, pitted and sliced

Directions

1. In a large bowl, add all the ingredients except avocado slices.
2. Cover the bowl and shake well to combine.
3. Serve with a topping of the avocado slices.

Los Angeles Lunch

Prep Time: 25 mins
Total Time: 25 mins

Servings per Recipe: 8
Calories	321 kcal
Fat	28.7 g
Carbohydrates	13.5g
Protein	4.9 g
Cholesterol	16 mg
Sodium	419 mg

Ingredients

- 1 avocado, peeled and pitted
- 1 tbsp lemon juice
- 1/2 C. mayonnaise
- 1/4 tsp hot pepper sauce
- 1/4 C. olive oil
- 1 clove garlic, peeled and minced
- 1/2 tsp salt
- 1 head romaine lettuce - rinsed, dried and torn into bite sized pieces
- 3 oz. Cheddar cheese, shredded
- 2 tomatoes, diced
- 2 green onions, chopped
- 1/4 (2.25 oz.) can pitted green olives
- 1 C. coarsely crushed corn chips

Directions

1. In a food processor, add avocado, garlic, mayonnaise, hot pepper sauce, olive oil, lemon juice and salt and pulse till smooth.
2. In a large bowl, mix together the romaine lettuce, tomatoes, olives, green onions, Cheddar cheese and corn chips.
3. Pour dressing over and toss to coat well.
4. Serve immediately.

QUINOA
Cucumber Salad

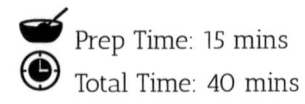

Prep Time: 15 mins
Total Time: 40 mins

Servings per Recipe: 2
Calories   313 kcal
Fat   19.9 g
Carbohydrates   26.6g
Protein   10.3 g
Cholesterol   28 mg
Sodium   620 mg

Ingredients

1/2 C. water
1/4 C. quinoa
4 leaves kale, chopped
1/2 avocado - peeled, pitted, and cut into cubes
1/2 tomato, cut into cubes

1/4 cucumber, peeled and cut into cubes
1/4 C. crumbled feta cheese
2 tbsp Italian-style salad dressing

Directions

1. In a pan, add the water and quinoa and bring to a boil.
2. Reduce the heat to medium-low and simmer, covered for about 15-20 minutes.
3. Drain the quinoa into a strainer and run under cold water to cool.
4. In a pan, arrange a steamer basket.
5. In the pan, add enough water to just below the bottom of the steamer and bring to a boil.
6. Add the kale and steam, covered for about 2-3 minutes.
7. Transfer the kale into a bowl and refrigerate for about 3-5 minutes.
8. In a bowl, mix together the quinoa, kale, avocado, cucumber, tomato.
9. Add the Italian dressing and gently, stir to combine.
10. Serve with a sprinkling of the feta cheese.

October
Avocado Salad

Prep Time: 10 mins
Total Time: 10 mins

Servings per Recipe:	1
Calories	251 kcal
Fat	17.3 g
Carbohydrates	26 g
Protein	3 g
Cholesterol	0 mg
Sodium	241 mg

Ingredients

1 C. baby spinach leaves
1 tbsp dried cranberries
1 tbsp chopped salted pecans
1/2 apple, cored and diced
1 tbsp diced red onion
2 tbsp grated carrot
1/4 avocado, peeled and diced
1 tbsp balsamic vinaigrette salad dressing

Directions

1. In a large bowl, add all the ingredients and toss to coat well.
2. Serve immediately.

SHRIMP and Avocado Picnic Salad

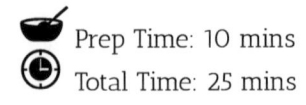

Prep Time: 10 mins
Total Time: 25 mins

Servings per Recipe: 3
Calories   460 kcal
Fat   25.6 g
Carbohydrates   29.4g
Protein   36.7 g
Cholesterol   250 mg
Sodium   566 mg

Ingredients

1 lb. medium shrimp - peeled and deveined
2 tbsp butter
2 lemons, juiced
2 heads butter lettuce
2 tomatoes, chopped
1 avocado - peeled, pitted and diced
2 stalks celery, chopped
1 cucumber, cleaned and chopped
1/2 C. shredded carrots
1/3 C. vinaigrette salad dressing

Directions

1. In a large sauté pan, melt the butter on medium heat and cook the shrimp and lemon juice, cook till the shrimp just turn pink.
2. Remove from the heat and drain well.
3. Tear the lettuce into bite-size pieces and place into a large bowl with the cooked shrimp, cucumber, carrots, tomatoes, avocado and celery and toss to coat.
4. Top with your favorite vinaigrette and serve.

Milanese Greek Style Salad

Prep Time: 10 mins
Total Time: 10 mins

Servings per Recipe: 6
Calories	248 kcal
Fat	21.3 g
Carbohydrates	9.2g
Protein	7.6 g
Cholesterol	12 mg
Sodium	1448 mg

Ingredients

- 1 (10 oz.) package mixed salad greens
- 1 ripe avocado - peeled, pitted and chopped
- 1 ripe tomato, chopped
- 1 (6 oz.) can black olives, drained
- 6 Greek pepperoncini peppers
- 1/4 C. olive oil
- 2 tsp white vinegar
- 2 tsp garlic salt
- 1 tsp dried oregano
- 1 tsp dried basil
- 3 oz. grated Parmesan cheese

Directions

1. In a large bowl, mix together the mixed greens, olives, avocado, tomato and pepperoncini peppers.
2. In a small bowl, add the vinegar, oil, basil, oregano and garlic salt and beat till well combined.
3. Pour the dressing over the salad and toss to coat well.
4. Serve with a sprinkling of the Parmesan.

FRESH
Dijon Garden Salad

🥣 Prep Time: 10 mins
🕐 Total Time: 10 mins

Servings per Recipe: 4	
Calories	326 kcal
Fat	30 g
Carbohydrates	10.5g
Protein	6.5 g
Cholesterol	13 mg
Sodium	562 mg

Ingredients

- 4 tbsp olive oil
- 2 tbsp white wine vinegar
- 1 tbsp Dijon mustard
- 1/2 tsp salt
- 1/2 tsp ground black pepper
- 1 pinch white sugar
- 1 tsp chopped fresh parsley
- 1 tsp fresh lemon juice
- 2 cloves garlic, chopped
- 1 avocados - peeled, pitted, and cubed
- 4 C. mixed salad greens
- 1/2 C. sliced almonds
- 2 oz. feta cheese, crumbled

Directions

1. In a large bowl, add the garlic, parsley, lemon juice, olive oil, white wine vinegar, mustard, sugar, salt and black pepper and beat till well combined.
2. Add the avocado and gently, stir to coat.
3. Add the salad greens and toss to coat well.
4. Serve immediately with a sprinkling of the almonds and feta cheese.

Alternative Fruit Salad

Prep Time: 15 mins
Total Time: 20 mins

Servings per Recipe: 6
Calories	628 kcal
Fat	47.5 g
Carbohydrates	52.4g
Protein	5.4 g
Cholesterol	0 mg
Sodium	416 mg

Ingredients

- 1 tsp white sugar
- 1 tbsp water
- 1/2 C. blanched slivered almonds
- 1 head leaf lettuce - rinsed, dried and torn into bite-size pieces
- 1 head romaine lettuce - rinsed, dried, and torn into bite-size pieces
- 2 bananas, peeled and sliced
- 1 avocado - pitted, peeled, and cubed
- 2 (11 oz.) cans mandarin oranges, drained
- 1 red onion, thinly sliced
- 1 C. vegetable oil
- 1/2 C. honey
- 1 tsp salt
- 1/3 C. distilled white vinegar
- 1 tsp dry mustard
- 1/2 tsp poppy seeds

Directions

1. In a skillet, mix together the water and sugar on medium heat.
2. Stir in the slivered almonds and cook till the almonds are brown, stirring continuously.
3. Remove from the heat.
4. In a large bowl, mix together the almonds, lettuce, onion, avocado and orange segments.
5. In a small bowl, add the honey, oil, vinegar, mustard and poppy seeds and beat till well combined.
6. Pour the dressing over the salad and toss to coat well.

SOUTHERN HONEY and Dijon Collard Green Salad

Prep Time: 30 mins
Total Time: 30 mins

Servings per Recipe: 4
Calories   421 kcal
Fat   27.8 g
Carbohydrates   43.8g
Protein   7.5 g
Cholesterol   0 mg
Sodium   394 mg

Ingredients

Salad:
4 collard leaves, trimmed and finely chopped
1/3 bunch kale, trimmed and chopped
1 head romaine lettuce, chopped
1/4 small head red cabbage, chopped
1 Bosc pear, cubed
1/2 Bermuda onion, finely diced
1/2 orange bell pepper, diced
1/2 Florida avocado - peeled, pitted, and diced
1/2 carrot, grated
5 cherry tomatoes, halved
7 walnut halves, crushed
2 tbsp raisins

Dressing:
6 tbsp olive oil
3 tbsp balsamic vinegar
1 tbsp wildflower honey
1 tbsp oregano, crushed
1 1/2 tsp chili powder
1 tsp Dijon mustard
1 clove garlic, minced
1/2 tsp salt
1/4 tsp crushed black peppercorns

Directions

1. In a large bowl, mix together all salad ingredients.
2. In a jar, add all dressing ingredients.
3. Seal the jar and shake well to combine.
4. Pour the dressing over salad and toss to coat well.
5. Serve immediately.

A Skinny Dinner

- Prep Time: 30 mins
- Total Time: 30 mins

Servings per Recipe: 3
Calories	495 kcal
Fat	36.8 g
Carbohydrates	7.3g
Protein	34.7 g
Cholesterol	144 mg
Sodium	579 mg

Ingredients

- 3/4 lb. boneless, skinless chicken breast halves
- Olive oil
- Salt and ground black pepper, to taste
- 1 (7.75 oz.) package DOLE(R) Extra Veggie(TM) with Grape Tomatoes
- 1 avocado, peeled and cubed
- 2 slices bacon, cooked, drained and crumbled
- 1 hard-cooked egg, peeled and chopped
- 1/4 C. crumbled blue cheese
- Bottled blue cheese dressing, to taste

Directions

1. Set your grill for medium-high heat and lightly, grease the grill grate.
2. Coat the chicken breast halves with the oil and season with the salt and black pepper.
3. Cook the chicken breast halves on grill for about 8-12 minutes, flipping once.
4. remove from grill and place the chicken breast halves onto a cutting board to cool slightly.
5. Then, cut chicken into thin strips.
6. In a large bowl, mix together the chicken strips, bacon, egg, salad blend, tomatoes from pouch, avocado and blue cheese.
7. Add the blue cheese dressing and toss to coat well.
8. Serve immediately.

ALFALFA and Lentil Lunchbox

Prep Time: 15 mins
Total Time: 30 mins

Servings per Recipe: 1
Calories 980.3
Fat 87.9g
Cholesterol 0.0mg
Sodium 71.3mg
Carbohydrates 50.2g 16
Protein 10.1g

Ingredients

2 C. mixed baby greens
1 C. baby spinach leaves
1/2 C. chopped fresh parsley
1/4-1/2 C. chopped fresh cilantro
1/2 C. alfalfa sprout
1/4 C. lentil sprouts
1/4 C. chopped cucumber
1/4 C. halved cherry tomatoes
1/4 C. chopped red bell pepper
1/2 C. snow peas, sliced thinly
2 garlic cloves, minced
1 - 2 scallion, chopped
1/4-1/2 C. thinly sliced of fresh mint
DRESSING
1 lemon, juice of
1/3 C. olive oil
1 tbsp honey
1/2 avocado, mashed
salt (optional)

Directions

1. In a large bowl, mix together the lettuces, bell peppers, snow peas, sprouts, cucumber, tomatoes, scallions, garlic, parsley, cilantro and mint.
2. In a small bowl, add the avocado and mash well.
3. Add the honey, lemon juice, oil and salt and beat till well combined.
4. Pour dressing over the salad and serve.

Simply Guacamole and Lime

Prep Time: 10 mins
Total Time: 40 mins

Servings per Recipe: 16
Calories	45 kcal
Fat	3.7 g
Carbohydrates	3.4g
Protein	0.7 g
Cholesterol	0 mg
Sodium	2 mg

Ingredients

- 2 avocados
- 1 small onion, finely chopped
- 1 clove garlic, minced
- 1 ripe tomato, chopped
- 1 lime, juiced
- salt and pepper to taste

Directions

1. Remove the skin from your avocados then place everything into a large dish. Mash the avocados a bit then add in your pepper, onion, salt, garlic, lime juice, and tomato. Mash the mix completely then add in some pepper, salt, and lime juice to your liking. Place everything in the fridge for at least 2 hours then serve.
2. Enjoy.

COOKOUT
Guacamole

Prep Time: 35 mins
Total Time: 1 hr 30 mins

Servings per Recipe: 12
Calories   128 kcal
Fat   11.1 g
Carbohydrates   7.9g
Protein   1.9 g
Cholesterol   4 mg
Sodium   88 mg

Ingredients

4 Hass avocados, halved and pitted
1/2 cup diced red onion
1 jalapeno pepper, seeded and minced
1/2 cup reduced-fat sour cream
2 tablespoons lime juice
1/2 teaspoon garlic salt

1/2 teaspoon hot pepper sauce (e.g. Tabasco(TM)), or to taste
12 cherry tomatoes, quartered
2 tablespoons chopped fresh cilantro, or to taste

Directions

1. Get a grill hot and coat the grilling grate with some oil. Place your avocado halves on the grill for cook them until they are somewhat brown and caramelized. Place the avocadoes to the side to lose their heat. Once everything is cool enough to handle take off the skin of the avocadoes and slice them into cubes.
2. Get a large dish and add in half of the avocadoes. Now add in your sour cream, onion, and jalapeno pepper. Begin to combine everything together with a masher evenly. Once the mix is smooth combine in your hot sauce, garlic salt, and lime juice. Begin to combine the mix again then place in your cilantro, cherry tomatoes, and the rest of the avocadoes and mash the mix again lightly.
3. Place everything in the fridge for 1 hours then serve.
4. Enjoy.

Tis' the Season for Guacamole

Prep Time: 20 mins
Total Time: 20 mins

Servings per Recipe: 12
Calories	144 kcal
Fat	10 g
Carbohydrates	15.2g
Protein	1.8 g
Cholesterol	0 mg
Sodium	166 mg

Ingredients

- 1/2 white onion, minced
- 4 serrano chili peppers, minced
- 1 teaspoon kosher salt
- 4 avocados - peeled, pitted and diced
- 2 1/2 tablespoons fresh lime juice
- 1 pear - peeled, cored and diced
- 1 cup seedless green grapes, halved
- 1 cup pomegranate seeds

Directions

1. Get a bowl combine evenly: salt, chili peppers, and onion. Then combine in the lime and prepared avocadoes. Combine the mix evenly then add in the pomegranate, grapes, and pears. Fold these fruits into the guacamole lightly but evenly then place everything in the fridge until it cold.
2. Enjoy.

SAN MIGUEL Inspired Guacamole

Prep Time: 15 mins
Total Time: 1 hr 15 mins

Servings per Recipe: 4
Calories   371 kcal
Fat   36.7 g
Carbohydrates   12.3g
Protein   2.9 g
Cholesterol   10 mg
Sodium   304 mg

Ingredients

2 ripe avocados, halved and pitted
1/4 cup hot salsa
1 tablespoon garlic powder
1/4 tablespoon chili powder
1 1/4 teaspoons hot pepper sauce, or to taste

1/2 cup mayonnaise

Directions

1. Place the flesh of your avocado into a bowl and begin to mix it with a masher. Combine in your hot sauce, salsa, chili powder, and garlic powder. Begin to combine everything again evenly.
2. Once the mix is smooth cover it with an even layer of mayo and combine it all again.
3. Now place a covering of plastic over everything then put the mix in the fridge to cool completely.
4. Enjoy.

Peach and Grape Guacamole

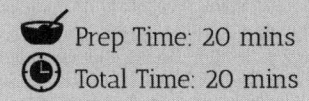

Prep Time: 20 mins
Total Time: 20 mins

Servings per Recipe: 8
Calories   48 kcal
Fat   3.7 g
Carbohydrates   4g
Protein   0.6 g
Cholesterol   0 mg
Sodium   2 mg

Ingredients

- 1 avocado - peeled, pitted, and diced
- 1 1/2 teaspoons minced red onion
- 1 teaspoon minced seeded serrano chili
- 12 red grapes, halved
- 1/2 cup fresh diced peaches
- salt to taste
- 2 tablespoons pomegranate seeds (optional)

Directions

1. Get a large serving dish then place into it your serrano and onion, then add in the avocado. Mash everything together evenly then combine in the peaches and the grapes. Combine everything again then taste the mix. Add some salt if you like then top everything with the pomegranate seeds.
2. Enjoy.

VEGETARIAN DREAM
Guacamole

🍲 Prep Time: 10 mins
🕒 Total Time: 10 mins

Servings per Recipe: 4
Calories   214 kcal
Fat   17.1 g
Carbohydrates   13.7 g
Protein   6.4 g
Cholesterol   0 mg
Sodium   595 mg

Ingredients

3/4 cup crumbled tofu
2 avocados - peeled and pitted, divided
1 lime, juiced
1 teaspoon salt
1/2 cup diced onion
3 tablespoons chopped fresh cilantro

2 roma (plum) tomatoes, diced
1 teaspoon minced garlic
1 pinch cayenne pepper (optional)

Directions

1. Add the avocados and tofu to a blender and work them until they are evenly combined.
2. Get a bowl and combine in it with a masher: salt, lime juice, and the rest of avocado. Once the mix is smooth then combine in the garlic, tofu mix, tomatoes, cilantro, and onion. Stir the mix nicely then combine in the cayenne.
3. Place a covering of plastic on the dish and put everything in the fridge for at 2 hours.
4. Enjoy.

Macho Mayo Guacamole

Prep Time: 10 mins
Total Time: 10 mins

Servings per Recipe: 20
Calories	21 kcal
Fat	2 g
Carbohydrates	0.9 g
Protein	0.2 g
Cholesterol	1 mg
Sodium	6 mg

Ingredients

1 Hass avocado, mashed
1 tablespoon mayonnaise (such as Hellman's(R)), or more to taste
freshly ground black pepper to taste
1 dash hot pepper sauce, or to taste (optional)

Directions

1. Get a big bowl and combine in your: hot sauce, avocado, black pepper, and mayo.
2. Mash the mix until it smooth then place a covering of plastic on the bowl and put in the fridge until it chilled.
3. Enjoy.

3-INGREDIENT
Guacamole

Prep Time: 10 mins
Total Time: 10 mins

Servings per Recipe: 4
Calories   231 kcal
Fat   20.8 g
Carbohydrates   11.6g
Protein   2.9 g
Cholesterol   13 mg
Sodium   267 mg

Ingredients

2 avocados - peeled, pitted, and mashed
1/2 cup sour cream
2 tablespoons dry Ranch-style dressing mix

Directions

1. Get a larger dish and simply mix the: ranch, sour cream, and avocado.
2. Place a covering of plastic on the bowl and put everything in the fridge for 30 mins.
3. Enjoy.

Bell Pepper Medley Guacamole

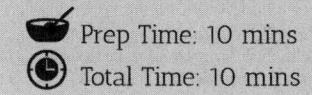

Prep Time: 10 mins
Total Time: 10 mins

Servings per Recipe: 3
Calories	371 kcal
Fat	29.8 g
Carbohydrates	28.9 g
Protein	5.7 g
Cholesterol	0 mg
Sodium	22 mg

Ingredients

- 3 avocados, peeled and mashed
- 1 red onion, minced
- 1 red bell pepper, chopped
- 1/2 yellow bell pepper, chopped
- 1 green bell pepper, chopped
- 1 fresh jalapeno pepper, chopped
- 1/3 cup chopped fresh cilantro
- 1 lime, juiced

Directions

1. Get a serving container combine: lime juice, avocados, cilantro, onion, jalapeno, and red, yellow, and green bell peppers.
2. Place a covering of plastic on the dish and put everything in the fridge until it is cold.
3. Enjoy.

I ♥ Guacamole

Prep Time: 10 mins
Total Time: 20 mins

Servings per Recipe: 6
Calories   94 kcal
Fat   7.7 g
Carbohydrates 6.8g
Protein   1.5 g
Cholesterol   0 mg
Sodium   6 mg

Ingredients

10 fresh tomatillos, husks removed
2 fresh jalapeno peppers, stems removed
1 bunch fresh cilantro, stems trimmed
1/3 cup fresh basil, diced finely
3 avocados, peeled and pitted
1 tablespoon garlic powder
salt to taste

Directions

1. Get your jalapenos and tomatillos boiling in water for 12 mins.
2. Now add the tomatillos and peppers to a food processor a little at a time to puree the mix completely. Once everything has been pureed nicely add in the avocados, cilantro, and basil and continue pureeing the mix for 60 secs.
3. As you are processing this mix add in some of the water from the boiling process to the mix smooth. Now add in some salt and garlic powder to your liking then puree the mix one last time.
4. Place everything in a container for serving.
5. Enjoy.

Coarse Garlic Guacamole

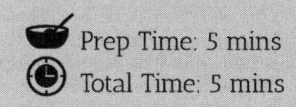

Prep Time: 5 mins
Total Time: 5 mins

Servings per Recipe: 8
Calories   68 kcal
Fat   6.2 g
Carbohydrates   3.6 g
Protein   0.9 g
Cholesterol   0 mg
Sodium   60 mg

Ingredients

- 2 (6 ounce) avocados, pitted peeled and mashed
- 1/4 teaspoon coarse garlic salt
- 1/2 tsp creole seasoning

Directions

1. Get a bowl, combine: garlic salt, avocado, and creole spice mix. Mash everything with a masher until it smooth.
2. Place the mix into a dish for serving with the pit in the middle. Put everything in the fridge with a covering of plastic until it is cold.
3. Enjoy.

FAJITA
Guacamole

Prep Time: 10 mins
Total Time: 10 mins

Servings per Recipe: 4
Calories	168 kcal
Fat	14.8 g
Carbohydrates	10.4g
Protein	2.3 g
Cholesterol	0 mg
Sodium	238 mg

Ingredients

2 avocados - peeled, pitted, and diced
2 green onions, chopped
1 tablespoon chopped fresh cilantro
1 teaspoon seasoned salt
1/2 tsp fajita seasoning
1 teaspoon ground black pepper

1 teaspoon garlic, minced
1/2 lime, juiced

Directions

1. Get a serving container and combine: lime juice, avocado, garlic, green onion, black pepper, cilantro, seasoned salt, and fajita spice.
2. Begin to mash everything together smoothly.
3. Enjoy.

Backroad Guacamole

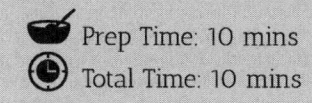

Prep Time: 10 mins
Total Time: 10 mins

Servings per Recipe: 9
Calories   109 kcal
Fat   9.9 g
Carbohydrates   5.3g
Protein   1.9 g
Cholesterol   10 mg
Sodium   254 mg

Ingredients

2 avocados - peeled, pitted, and mashed
4 teaspoons lime juice
1/2 cup salsa
3 ounces cream cheese, softened
1/4 tsp rosemary

1 clove garlic, pressed
1/ teaspoon salt
1/2 teaspoon hot pepper sauce

Directions

1. Get a serving container combine: hot sauce, avocado, salt, lime juice, garlic, salsa, rosemary, and cream cheese.
2. Work the mix completely with a masher then place everything into a blender. Continue to pulse the mix until it is evenly combined.
3. Place everything into a serving container again.
4. Enjoy.

BLACK AND YELLOW
Guacamole with Corn

Prep Time: 20 mins
Total Time: 20 mins

Servings per Recipe: 8
Calories   170 kcal
Fat   11.3 g
Carbohydrates 16.6 g
Protein   3.8 g
Cholesterol   0 mg
Sodium   261 mg

Ingredients

1/2 red bell pepper, minced
1/2 red onion, minced
2 cloves garlic, minced
1/2 (15.25 ounce) can sweet corn, drained
1/2 (15 ounce) can black beans, drained and rinsed
3 ripe avocados, peeled, pitted and sliced

2 tablespoons fresh lime juice
1/4 teaspoon salt
1 pinch ground black pepper, or to taste
1/2 cup chopped fresh cilantro, or more to taste (optional)

Directions

1. Get a bowl, combine: avocado pieces, bell pepper, black beans, red onion, sweet corn, and garlic. Begin to work the mix with a masher then combine your cilantro, black pepper, salt, and lime. Continue to mash everything for 2 more mins.
2. Enjoy.

Honolulu County Guacamole

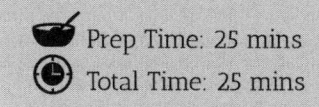

Prep Time: 25 mins
Total Time: 25 mins

Servings per Recipe: 6
Calories   156 kcal
Fat   10.1 g
Carbohydrates   18.7g
Protein   2.2 g
Cholesterol   0 mg
Sodium   8 mg

Ingredients

2 ripe avocados - peeled, halved and pitted, mashed
1/4 whole fresh pineapple - peeled, cored, and diced
1 mango - peeled, seeded and diced
2 small tomatoes, diced
1/4 red onion, diced
1/3 cucumber, diced (optional)
1 teaspoon chopped fresh cilantro, or to taste
2 limes, juiced
1 pinch garlic powder
salt and ground black pepper to taste

Directions

1. Combine the following with your mashed avocados: black pepper, pineapple, salt, mango, garlic powder, tomatoes, lime juice, red onion, cilantro, cucumber. Mash the mix with a masher until it even and smooth.
2. Place a covering of plastic on the dish and put everything in the fridge until it is chilled.
3. Enjoy.

SWEET SMOKED
Guacamole

Prep Time: 10 mins
Total Time: 10 mins

Servings per Recipe: 8
Calories	166 kcal
Fat	14.8 g
Carbohydrates	9.9g
Protein	2.2 g
Cholesterol	0 mg
Sodium	298 mg

Ingredients

4 avocados - peeled, pitted, and chopped
1 roma tomato, cut in half
1/2 red onion, roughly chopped
1/2 tsp sweet smoked paprika
2 tablespoons lemon juice

1/2 jalapeno pepper, seeded and minced (optional)
1 teaspoon salt

Directions

1. Add the following to a food processor: salt, avocados, paprika, tomato, jalapenos, lemon juice, and onion. Puree the mix completely until the mix achieves a consistency of your liking.
2. Enjoy.

Sesame Thai Guacamole

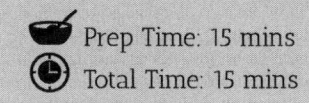

Prep Time: 15 mins
Total Time: 15 mins

Servings per Recipe: 6
Calories   254 kcal
Fat   20.9 g
Carbohydrates   19.1g
Protein   3.3 g
Cholesterol   0 mg
Sodium   1175 mg

Ingredients

3 large avocados, peeled and pitted
1 small red onion, chopped
1 mango - peeled, pitted, and chopped
1 lime, juiced
1/4 tsp sesame seeds
1 tablespoon minced garlic
1 tablespoon salt
3 tablespoons chopped fresh cilantro

Directions

1. Get a bowl for your avocados and mash them with a masher until they are chunky. Then combine in your cilantro, onion, salt, sesame, garlic, lime juice, and mango. Continue to mash everything together completely.
2. Place the mix in the fridge for 30 mins.
3. Enjoy.

GUACAMOLE
Dream

Prep Time: 15 mins
Total Time: 45 mins

Servings per Recipe: 16
Calories   90 kcal
Fat   7.9 g
Carbohydrates   5.4g
Protein   1.2 g
Cholesterol   1 mg
Sodium   11 mg

Ingredients

3 large avocados - peeled, pitted, and diced, mashed
1 tomato, seeded and chopped
2 green onions, finely chopped
1/2 lime, juiced
1 tablespoon salsa, or more to taste
1 clove garlic, minced
1 teaspoon sour cream
1 teaspoon white vinegar
1/2 teaspoon cayenne pepper
1/4 teaspoon cumin
salt and ground black pepper to taste

Directions

1. Combine your cumin, tomato, cayenne, green onions, vinegar, lime juice, sour cream, salsa, and garlic with the mashed avocados and continue to combine everything evenly. Combine in your black pepper and salt, and place everything in the fridge 1 hour, covered.
2. Enjoy.

New-Age Guacamole

Prep Time: 10 mins
Total Time: 10 mins

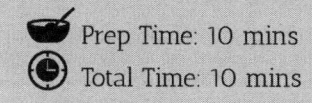

Servings per Recipe: 4
Calories   90 kcal
Fat   7.5 g
Carbohydrates   5.8g
Protein   2.2 g
Cholesterol   0 mg
Sodium   331 mg

Ingredients

- 1 avocado, halved and pitted
- 2 tablespoons chopped onion
- 1 1/2 tablespoons hot salsa
- 1 tablespoon nutritional yeast
- 1/2 teaspoon salt, or to taste

Directions

1. Remove the avocado from its skin and pit then begin to mash it in a serving dish then combine your salsa, and onion and stir everything together completely. Top the mix with your yeast and salt and stir again.
2. Enjoy.

GUACAMOLE
for August

Prep Time: 20 mins
Total Time: 50 mins

Servings per Recipe: 8
Calories   278 kcal
Fat   22.3 g
Carbohydrates   21.2g
Protein   3.9 g
Cholesterol   0 mg
Sodium   572 mg

Ingredients

4 avocados - peeled, pitted, and sliced
2 tomatoes, seeded and chopped
1/2 small red onion, chopped
1/2 cucumber, sliced
1 small fresh jalapeno pepper, seeded and diced
1 (15.25 ounce) can whole kernel corn, drained

1/2 teaspoon garlic salt
salt and black pepper to taste
juice of 1 fresh lime
1/4 cup extra virgin olive oil

Directions

1. Get a large serving container and combine in your corn, avocados, jalapenos, tomatoes, cucumber, and red onion. Stir the mix completely but do not mash then coat everything with the following spices and stir again: black pepper, salt, and garlic salt.
2. Get a small container then evenly mix in the container your olive oil and lime juice. Top your avocado mix with the oil mix then place everything in the fridge for 2 hours.
3. Enjoy.

Tropical Guacamole

Prep Time: 20 mins
Total Time: 20 mins

Servings per Recipe: 8
Calories   198 kcal
Fat   14.9 g
Carbohydrates   19 g
Protein   2.5 g
Cholesterol   0 mg
Sodium   49 mg

Ingredients

2 tablespoons minced white onion
2 limes, juiced
2 serrano chili peppers, or to taste
2 limes, juiced
sea salt to taste
4 ripe avocados, peeled and pitted
1/4 cup chopped fresh cilantro
1 large mango - peeled, seeded, and chopped

Directions

1. Get a container then mix in the juice of 2 limes and onion. Let the mix stand for 3 hours then discard the remaining juices. Leave the onions to stand.
2. Add the following to a blender and puree it: salt, remaining lime juice, and serrano peppers. Once the mix is completely smooth then add in the flesh of 1 avocado. Puree the mix completely then add another avocado and continue to puree the mix in this fashion, one avocado at a time, to keep everything smooth and manageable.
3. Place everything into a large dish then add in your mango, cilantro, and onion and stir the mix evenly.
4. Enjoy immediately.

2-PEPPER Guacamole

Prep Time: 15 mins
Total Time: 15 mins

Servings per Recipe: 8
Calories   170 kcal
Fat   14.8 g
Carbohydrates   10.7g
Protein   2.4 g
Cholesterol   0 mg
Sodium   9 mg

Ingredients

4 avocados - peeled, pitted, and chopped
1/2 cup chopped red onion
2 habanero peppers, seeded and minced (wear gloves), or to taste
2 cloves garlic, minced
1 tablespoon lime juice
1 teaspoon cayenne pepper
4 sprigs cilantro, chopped, or to taste
1/2 large tomato, seeded and finely diced

Directions

1. Add the following to a blender and process it completely: cilantro, avocadoes, cayenne, red onions, lime juice, habanero, and garlic. Process the mix until it is completely smooth then place everything into a serving dish.
2. Add in the tomatoes and stir everything completely.
3. Enjoy.

Kiwi Guacamole

Prep Time: 10 mins
Total Time: 10 mins

Servings per Recipe: 6
Calories   174 kcal
Fat   14 g
Carbohydrates   13.7g
Protein   2.3 g
Cholesterol   0 mg
Sodium   9 mg

Ingredients

2 large avocados, peeled and pitted
1 cup chopped kiwi
1/4 cup chopped fresh cilantro
1/4 cup chopped green onion
1 tablespoon fresh lime juice
1 serrano chili pepper, minced (optional)
salt and ground black pepper to taste

Directions

1. Get a dish for serving and place in your avocados and begin to work them with a masher until they are smooth. Now combine in the following: pepper, kiwi, salt, cilantro, serrano, lime juice, and green onion.
2. Continue to process the mix with your masher until it is a consistency of liking then serve.
3. Enjoy.

ANNABELLE'S
Guacamole

Prep Time: 10 mins
Total Time: 10 mins

Servings per Recipe: 8
Calories	111 kcal
Fat	9.4 g
Carbohydrates	4.9 g
Protein	3.4 g
Cholesterol	79 mg
Sodium	85 mg

Ingredients

- 2 avocados - peeled, pitted, and mashed
- 3 hard-boiled eggs
- 2 tablespoons lemon juice
- 1 teaspoon lemon pepper
- salt to taste (optional)

Directions

1. Get a bowl for serving then combine in your eggs and avocado. Process the mix evenly with your masher then combine in your lemon pepper, and lemon juice.
2. Add in some salt and continue to work the mix until it is smooth.
3. Enjoy.

Mediterranean Guacamole

Prep Time: 20 mins
Total Time: 55 mins

Servings per Recipe: 10
Calories   22 kcal
Fat   0.3 g
Carbohydrates   4.1g
Protein   1.9 g
Cholesterol   1 mg
Sodium   10 mg

Ingredients

- 1 1/2 pounds asparagus, cut into small pieces
- 1 tablespoon fat-free Greek-style yogurt
- 1 tablespoon lime juice
- 1/4 cup chopped fresh cilantro
- 3 green onions, thinly sliced
- 1/2 jalapeno pepper, minced
- 1 tablespoon minced garlic
- 1 tomato, diced
- 1/2 teaspoon Worcestershire sauce
- 1 dash hot pepper sauce
- salt and ground black pepper to taste

Directions

1. Get a steamer insert and put it into a large soup pot. Add in about 3 inches of hot water and get everything boiling. Place your spears of asparagus into the steamer insert, place a lid on the pot, and let everything steam for 7 mins. Place the spears into a blender and process them until they are smooth.
2. Get a bowl, combine in: hot sauce, yogurt, Worcestershire, lime juice, tomato, cilantro, garlic, jalapeno, and green onions. Stir the mix until it is smooth then add in your asparagus and stir everything again. Add in some pepper and salt then place everything in the fridge until it cool.
3. Enjoy.

CALIFORNIA
x Florida Popsicles

 Prep Time: 10 mins
 Total Time: 2 hrs 10 mins

Servings per Recipe: 6
Calories   103
Fat   6.7g
Cholesterol   0mg
Sodium   77mg
Carbohydrates   11.3g
Protein   0.8g

Ingredients

1 avocado, peeled and pitted
1/2 C. coconut milk
1/4 C. agave nectar
1/4 C. lime juice

2 tsp. vanilla extract
1/4 tsp. salt

Directions

1. In a food processor, add all the ingredients and pulse until smooth.
2. Transfer the mixture into Popsicle molds evenly.
3. Now, insert 1 Popsicle stick into each mold and place in the freezer for about 2-3 hours.
4. Carefully, remove the popsicles from molds and enjoy.

California Paletas

Prep Time: 5 mins
Total Time: 6 hrs 5 mins

Servings per Recipe: 6
Calories   142
Fat   7.4g
Cholesterol   0mg
Sodium   5mg
Carbohydrates   20.8g
Protein   1g

Ingredients

- 1/2 C. agave nectar
- 1 C. warm water
- 2 avocados, diced
- 3 tbsp. fresh lime juice
- 1 pinch salt

Directions

1. In a bowl, add the agave nectar and warm water and mix until well combined.
2. In a food processor, add the agave nectar mixture and remaining ingredients and pulse until smooth.
3. Transfer the mixture into Popsicle molds evenly.
4. Now, insert 1 Popsicle stick into each mold and place in the freezer for about 6 hours.
5. Carefully, remove the popsicles from molds and enjoy.

AVOCADO Arepas

Prep Time: 35 mins
Total Time: 45 mins

Servings per Recipe: 6
Calories 716.0
Fat 25.9g
Cholesterol 48.4mg
Sodium 1173.7mg
Carbohydrates 98.3g
Protein 29.3g

Ingredients

Filling
1 lb. boneless skinless chicken breast, poached, cooled and shredded
1/4 C. chopped cilantro
2 tbsp mayonnaise
1/2 tsp salt
ground black pepper
4 avocados, pitted, peeled and mashed
1/2 lime, juice

Dough
4 C. cold water
3/4 tbsp salt
1 1/2 lb. Venezuelan masa harina
oil

Directions

1. For the filling: in a bowl, add all the ingredients and mix well.
2. Cover the bowl and place in the fridge until cooking.
3. For the dough: in a bowl, add the water and salt and mix.
4. Gradually, add the cornmeal, mixing continuously until well combined.
5. With your hands, knead until a soft dough forms.
6. Make 8 balls from the dough and then gently pat each into a disc.
7. Set your grill for medium heat and lightly, grease the grill grate.
8. Grease a skillet with a thin layer of the oil and place over high heat until heated through.
9. Add the arepas and cook about 1 1/2 minutes per side.
10. Now, transfer the arepas onto the grill and cook for about 10 minutes, flipping once half way through.
11. Carefully, split the arepas in half and then remove some of the middle.
12. Stuff the arepas with the chicken mixture evenly and enjoy hot.

Southwest Avocado Blend

Prep Time: 1 min
Total Time: 3 mins

Servings per Recipe: 1
Calories   283.0
Fat   23.8g
Cholesterol   0.0mg
Sodium   951.0mg
Carbohydrates   20.2g
Protein   4.2g

Ingredients

1 ripe avocado, peeled, cored and chopped
3/4 C. water
1 tsp. lime zest
3 tbsp. lime juice
1/2 tsp. cumin
1/2 tsp. salt
1/2 tsp. pepper
2 green onions, chopped
1 clove garlic

Directions

1. In a food processor, add all the ingredients and pulse until well combined.
2. Enjoy the dressing over your favorite salad

FLORIDA
Avocado Lunch Box

🥣 Prep Time: 20 mins
🕐 Total Time: 20 mins

Servings per Recipe: 8
Calories 218.9
Fat 13.5g
Cholesterol 0.0mg
Sodium 10.3mg
Carbohydrates 25.1g
Protein 1.6g

Ingredients

1/3 C. olive oil
1/3 C. vinegar
1/3 C. orange juice
1/3 C. sugar
salt and pepper
1 head iceberg lettuce, shredded
2 C. of fresh ripe pineapple chunks
1 medium red onion, sliced thin
1 large Florida avocado, peeled and sliced
fresh lime

Directions

1. Get a food processor: Blend in it the olive oil, vinegar, orange juice, and sugar smooth to make the dressing.
2. Get a mixing bowl: Mix in it the lettuce, pineapple, and red onion.
3. Drizzle over it the dressing. Toss them to coat. Kay the avocado slices on top.
4. Serve your salad right away.
5. Enjoy.

Red Avocado Salsa

🥣 Prep Time: 45 mins
🕐 Total Time: 45 mins

Servings per Recipe: 6
Calories   84.7
Fat   7.1g
Cholesterol   0.0mg
Sodium   5.9mg
Carbohydrates   3.8g
Protein   0.7g

Ingredients

1/2 red onion, sliced
1 C. red wine vinegar
1 Florida avocados
1 tbsp highest-quality extra-virgin olive oil
salt and black pepper

Directions

1. To make the onion:
2. Stir the onion slices with vinegar in a zip lock bag. Seal it. Let it sit for 35 min.
3. Drain the onion. Reserve few tbsp of the vinegar.
4. To make the salad:
5. Get a serving plate: Lay in it the avocado slices followed by the onion slices.
6. Pour over them the olive oil with the reserved vinegar.
7. Sprinkle a pinch of salt on top then serve your salad right away.
8. Enjoy.

SPICY Green Hummus

Prep Time: 15 mins
Total Time: 1 hr 15 mins

Servings per Recipe: 13
Calories 50.1
Fat 2.5g
Cholesterol 0.0mg
Sodium 66.3mg
Carbohydrates 6.2g
Protein 1.3g

Ingredients

- 1 medium avocado, pitted and chopped
- 1 C. canned chickpeas, drained
- 1/3 C. chopped onion
- 2 large garlic cloves, minced
- 3 tsp lemon juice
- 1 tsp hot sauce
- 1 tsp ground cumin
- Ritz crackers

Directions

1. Get a food processor: Combine in it the avocado with chickpeas, onion, garlic, lemon juice, hot sauce and cumin.
2. Process them until they become smooth.
3. Pour the hummus in a serving bowl and cover it. Let it rest in the fridge for at least 60 min.
4. Serve your hummus with a sandwich, roasted meat or some crackers.
5. Enjoy.

Salad Cubana

Prep Time: 15 mins
Total Time: 15 mins

Servings per Recipe: 2
Calories   731.0
Fat   69.3g
Cholesterol   0.0mg
Sodium   74.0mg
Carbohydrates   28.1g
Protein   6.6g

Ingredients

- 1 head lettuce, torn into bite size
- 2 tomatoes, sliced
- 1 onion, sliced in rounds
- 6 radishes, sliced
- 1 avocado, sliced
- Dressing
- 3 garlic cloves, minced
- 1/4 C. vinegar
- 1/4 C. lime juice
- salt
- pepper
- 1/2 C. olive oil

Directions

1. To make the dressing:
2. Get a food processor: Combine in it all the dressing ingredients. Blend them smooth.
3. To make the salad:
4. Lay the lettuce in a serving plate. Lay over it the tomato slices with followed by radishes, onion rings and avocado slices on top.
5. Drizzle the dressing all over the salad. Serve it right away.
6. Enjoy.

LATIN
Bruschetta

Prep Time: 10 mins
Total Time: 10 mins

Servings per Recipe: 6
Calories	258.7
Fat	19.7g
Cholesterol	0.0mg
Sodium	467.9mg
Carbohydrates	19.6g
Protein	3.4g

Ingredients

2 tbsp lemon juice
2 tbsp red wine vinegar
3 garlic cloves, minced
3/4 tsp salt
1/2 tsp red pepper flakes
1/2 tsp dried oregano
1/4 tsp ground black pepper
1/4 C. olive oil
1/4 C. chopped cilantro
1/4 C. chopped parsley
2 avocados, peeled, pitted and cubed
6 slices bread

Directions

1. In a bowl, add the garlic, vinegar, lemon juice, oregano salt, red pepper flakes and black pepper and mix until well combined.
2. Add the oil and beat until well combined.
3. Add the parsley and cilantro and stir to combine.
4. Gently, fold in the avocado cubes.
5. To the toast slices with the avocado mixture and serve.

Burgers
Santa Domingo

Prep Time: 10 mins
Total Time: 20 mins

Servings per Recipe: 1
Calories   441.6
Fat   22.7g
Cholesterol   66.9mg
Sodium   760.4mg
Carbohydrates   39.4g
Protein   20.2g

Ingredients

- 1 (10 oz.) packages angel hair coleslaw mix
- 1 lb. beef ground round, crumbled
- 1 large egg, lightly beaten
- 1/4 C. chopped cilantro
- 1/4 C. finely chopped onion
- 1 tsp chili powder
- 1 tsp ground cumin
- 1 tsp seasoning salt
- 2 tsp lime juice
- 1/4 C. ketchup
- 1/4 C. mayonnaise
- 12 dinner rolls, split
- 1 avocado, pitted, peeled and sliced
- 12 slices tomatoes
- 1 (14 oz.) round Chihuahua queso Blanco cheese, sliced

Directions

1. Set your grill for medium-high heat and lightly, grease the grill grate.
2. In a large pan, add the water over medium-high heat and bring to a boil.
3. Stir in the cabbage and immediately remove from the heat.
4. Keep the pan aside for about 5 minutes. Drain the cabbage well and keep aside.
5. In a large bowl, add the beef, onion, cilantro, egg, lime juice, cumin, chili powder and seasoned salt and mix until well combined.
6. Make 12 equal sized small patties from the beef mixture.
7. Cook the patties onto the grill, covered for about 2-3 minutes per side.
8. Meanwhile, in a small bowl, add the mayonnaise and ketchup and mix until well combined
9. Spread the ketchup mixture over the cut sides of each roll evenly.
10. Arrange the hot burgers onto the bottom half of each roll, followed by the cheese, avocado, tomato and cabbage.
11. Cover with top half of the roll and serve.

CHICKEN Cutlets Chimichurri

🥣 Prep Time: 4 hrs
🕐 Total Time: 4 hrs 15 mins

Servings per Recipe: 4
Calories 1007.7
Fat 82.0g
Cholesterol 100.4mg
Sodium 1065.2mg
Carbohydrates 31.4g
Protein 38.5g

Ingredients

4 large boneless skinless chicken breast halves
1 C. prepared chimichurri sauce
2 tbsp canola oil
1 medium red onion, peeled and cut into strips
salt and pepper
4 sandwich buns, split
nonstick cooking spray
4 slices Monterey Jack cheese
1 ripe avocado, sliced
1 C. lettuce leaf

Sauce:
2 C. loosely packed flat leaf parsley sprigs
1/2 C. loosely packed cilantro stem
1 Serrano Chile, coarsely chopped
2 tbsp red wine vinegar
1 tbsp minced garlic
1 1/4 tsp kosher salt
1/4 tsp pepper
1 C. olive oil

Directions

1. For the chimichurri sauce: in a food processor, add the garlic, cilantro, parsley, Chile, vinegar, salt and pepper and pulse until finely chopped.
2. While the motor is running, slowly add the oil and 1 tbsp of water and pulse until smooth nicely.
3. For the chimichurri sandwiches: in a large zip lock bag, place the chicken and 3/4 C. of the chimichurri sauce.
4. Seal the bag and shake to coat well.
5. Refrigerate to marinate overnight.
6. Set your grill for medium-high heat and lightly, grease the grill grate.
7. Remove the chicken from bag and discard the marinade.
8. Cook the chicken onto the grill for about 2-4 minutes per side.
9. In the last minute of the cooking, place 1 cheese slice on top of each breast.

10. Remove the chicken from the grill and keep aside for about 5 minutes.
11. In a large skillet, heat the canola oil over medium heat and sauté the onion for about 8-10 minutes.
12. Stir in the salt and pepper and remove from the heat.
13. Place the remaining chimichurri sauce onto the cut side of each bun evenly.
14. Top each bun with a chicken breast, followed by the onions, avocado and lettuce.
15. Cover each with top bun and serve.

SONOMA
Black Bean Tacos

🥣 Prep Time: 30 mins
🕐 Total Time: 1 hr 15 mins

Servings per Recipe: 4
Calories   764.7
Fat   46.3g
Cholesterol   0.0mg
Sodium   1249.8mg
Carbohydrates   74.6g
Protein   15.9g

Ingredients

Brown Rice:
2 tbsp olive oil
1 onion, finely chopped
1/2 tsp sea salt
1 tomatoes, finely chopped
1/2 C. brown rice
1 C. vegetable broth
Sauce:
1 C. cilantro
1/2 C. Italian parsley
1/2 C. olive oil
1/4 C. lime juice
4 garlic cloves
2 tbsp agave syrup
1/2 tsp ground cumin
1 tsp sea salt
1/2 tsp ground black pepper

Filling:
2 tbsp olive oil
8 oz. cremini mushrooms, trimmed and sliced
1 (15 oz.) cans black beans, rinsed and drained
1 (8 oz.) packages flour tortillas
Finishing's:
sour cream
chopped tomato
sliced onion
shredded lettuce
diced avocado

Directions

1. For the tomato rice: heat the oil in a medium pan over medium-high heat and sauté the onions with the salt until tender.
2. Stir in the rice, tomato and broth and bring to a rolling boil over high heat.
3. Immediately, reduce the heat to low.
4. Cover the pan and simmer until all the liquid absorbs.
5. Remove from the heat and keep aside, covered for about 15 minutes.
6. For the chimichurri sauce: in a food processor, add the garlic, parsley, cilantro, agave nectar, lime juice, oil, cumin, salt and pepper and pulse until well blended.

7. In a small bowl, reserve half of the chimichurri sauce and keep aside.
8. For the filling: heat the oil in a large skillet over medium-high heat and cook the mushrooms for about 3-4 minutes.
9. Stir in the remaining chimichurri sauce and black beans and cook until heated completely.
10. Place the tomato rice in each tortilla, followed by the mushroom mixture, reserved chimichurri sauce, your favorite topping and sour cream.
11. Fold each tortilla like a burrito and serve.

TOPPED
Seafood Tacos

Prep Time: 3 mins
Total Time: 10 mins

Servings per Recipe: 2
Calories	316.4
Fat	18.8 g
Cholesterol	7.2 mg
Sodium	152.2 mg
Carbohydrates	32.3 g
Protein	8.3 g

Ingredients

Sauce
1 large avocado, chopped
1/2 C. water
1/4 C. loosely packed cilantro
1/2-1 large pickled jalapeno pepper, seeded
1 tbsp fresh limes
1 large garlic clove
kosher salt
black pepper
Marinade
1 tbsp olive oil
1/2 limes, zest
1 tbsp limes
1 garlic clove, minced
kosher salt
pepper
Tacos
4 -6 large sea scallops
olive oil
1/2 C. green cabbage, sliced
1/4 C. red onion, sliced
1 -1 1/2 tbsp cilantro, chopped
4 corn tortillas

Directions

1. Get a food processor: Combine it all the sauce ingredients. Blend them smooth to make the sauce.
2. Get a mixing bowl: Whisk in it the marinade ingredients.
3. Cut each scallop in half. Stir into it into the marinade.
4. Put on the lid and chill it in the fridge for 16 min. Get a mixing bowl: Combine in it the cabbage with onion and cilantro.
5. Place a large pan over medium heat. Hat in it the olive oil.
6. Drain the scallops from the marinade. Cook them in the hot oil for 40 sec to 1 min on each side.
7. Heat the tortillas in a pan or a microwave. Place them on serving plates.
8. Top each one of them with the cabbage salad, scallops, and avocado sauce.
9. Wrap your tortillas then toast them in a grill pan or a grill. Serve them warm.
10. Enjoy.

American Shrimp Flatbreads

Prep Time: 15 mins
Total Time: 30 mins

Servings per Recipe: 4
Calories   116.7
Fat   9.2 g
Cholesterol   17.9 mg
Sodium   330.1 mg
Carbohydrates   3.2 g
Protein   5.7 g

Ingredients

- 1/2 C. tomato sauce
- 2 C. Traditional Mashed Potatoes
- 1 tbsp milk
- 1/4 C. alfredo sauce
- 2 tsp cilantro, chopped
- 1/16 tsp salt
- 1 pinch ground pepper
- 4 pieces naan bread
- 16 pieces shrimp, peeled and deveined
- 1 tbsp extra virgin olive oil
- 1/8 tsp cumin
- 1/16 tsp salt
- 1 pinch ground pepper
- 2 pieces avocados
- 2 slices swiss cheese
- 2 slices American cheese

Directions

1. Before you do anything, preheat the oven to 350 F.
2. Place a large saucepan over medium heat. Combine in it the potatoes with milk.
3. Heat them while stirring until they become creamy.
4. Pour the mixture into a greased baking dish. Pour over it the alfredo sauce.
5. Bake it for 8 to 12 min until it starts bubbling.
6. Garnish it with cilantro, a pinch of salt and pepper. Place it aside to cool down for a while.
7. Place a small pan over medium heat. Heat in it the oil.
8. Stir in it the shrimp with cumin, a pinch of salt and pepper.
9. Cook them for 3 to 5 min while stirring.
10. Slice the naan bread in half. Spoon to it the tomato sauce, avocado, mashed potato, grilled shrimp, American cheese and Swiss cheese.
11. Place the sandwiches on a baking sheet. Broil them in the oven for 3 to 4 min. Serve them warm.
12. Enjoy.

CEVICHE
Cups

Prep Time: 10 mins
Total Time: 10 mins

Servings per Recipe: 4
Calories 278.8
Fat 15.1g
Cholesterol 37.4mg
Sodium 346.6mg
Carbohydrates 15.1g
Protein 23.6g

Ingredients

2 (6 oz.) cans albacore tuna in water, drained
1/2 C. sweet onion, diced
1 large tomatoes, seeded and diced
1 small cucumber, peeled and diced
1/4 C. cilantro,
1 - 2 serrano chili, diced
2 - 3 limes, juice

1 tbsp olive oil
salt
pepper
1 large avocado, diced
8 tostadas

Directions

1. Get a mixing bowl: Stir in it the tuna, onion, tomato, cucumber, and cilantro.
2. Pour over them the lime juice, olive oil, salt, and pepper. Toss them to coat.
3. Stir in the serrano chilies, followed by avocado.
4. Spoon your ceviche into tostadas then serve them right away.
5. Enjoy.

West Indian Ceviche

Prep Time: 40 mins
Total Time: 42 mins

Servings per Recipe: 4
Calories	470.4
Fat	13.0g
Cholesterol	265.0mg
Sodium	1131.5mg
Carbohydrates	61.3g
Protein	42.5g

Ingredients

- 1/2 lb. salmon, cubed
- 1 lb. of shell-less shrimp
- 1 big mango, peeled and diced
- 1/2 red onion, diced
- 4 small tomatoes, peeled and diced
- 1 chile serrano pepper, chopped
- cilantro, to desire
- 1 avocado, diced
- 20 limes, juice

Directions

1. Get a mixing bowl: Stir in it the shrimp and salmon with lime juice. Season them with a pinch of salt.
2. Cover the bowl and place it in the fridge for 2 h 30 min.
3. Once the time is up, drain the shrimp and salmon. Transfer them to another mixing bowl.
4. Add the remaining ingredients and toss them to coat.
5. Spoon your ceviche into serving glasses and serve them.
6. Enjoy.

NAKED Ceviche

Prep Time: 20 mins
Total Time: 1 hr 20 mins

Servings per Recipe: 8
Calories   231.4
Fat   12.6g
Cholesterol   129.6mg
Sodium   208.7mg
Carbohydrates   12.5g
Protein   19.5g

Ingredients

1 1/2 lbs. raw shrimp, peeled and cleaned
5 limes, juice
2 tbsp minced jalapenos, divided
1/4 C. minced red onion, divided
1/4 tsp salt
1 cucumber, peeled, seeded, and diced
3 avocados, diced
2 tomatoes, seeded and diced
1 bunch fresh cilantro, chopped
tortilla chips

Directions

1. Get a mixing bowl: Stir in it the shrimp with lime juice, 1 tbsp jalapeno, 2 tbsp red onion, and a pinch of salt.
2. Cover it and place it in the fridge for 60 min.
3. Once the time is up, stir in the cucumber, avocado, tomato, and cilantro.
4. Adjust the seasoning of your ceviche then serve it with some chips.
5. Enjoy.

Bar Harbor Ceviche

Prep Time: 30 mins
Total Time: 4 hrs 30 mins

Servings per Recipe: 4
Calories   323.9
Fat   14.8g
Cholesterol   36.5mg
Sodium   322.4mg
Carbohydrates   43.8g
Protein   16.9g

Ingredients

- 1/2 lobster
- 1/2 lb. sea scallops, cleaned and patted dry
- 4 oranges, juiced
- 4 lemons, juiced
- 4 limes, juiced
- 1 Bermuda onion, sliced
- 2 small tomatoes, chopped
- 3 tbsp fresh cilantro, chopped
- 1/2 small habanero, chopped
- 1/4 C. Spanish olive oil
- 1/4 C. ketchup
- salt & ground pepper
- avocado
- plantain chips

Directions

1. Bring a large saucepan of water to a boil. Cook in it the lobster for 6 to 7 min.
2. Drain it and place it in a bowl of ice-cold water. Drain it and transfer it to a mixing bowl.
3. Add to it the orange, lemon, and lime juice, onions, tomatoes, cilantro, habanero, olive oil, ketchup, salt, and pepper.
4. Toss them to coat. Cover the bowl with a plastic wrap and chill it in the fridge for 4 to 5 h.
5. Once the time is up, strain the ceviche then serve it with some avocado.
6. Enjoy.

CRUNCHY Crab Ceviche

Prep Time: 10 mins
Total Time: 20 mins

Servings per Recipe: 6
Calories 642.6
Fat 20.1g
Cholesterol 264.0mg
Sodium 1145.5mg
Carbohydrates 68.9g
Protein 47.5g

Ingredients

canola oil
18 (5 inches) tortillas
1 1/2 lbs. medium cooked shrimp, peeled, deveined and chopped
3/4 lb. lump crabmeat
1/4 C. lemon juice
2 tbsp chopped cilantro
1 large cucumber, peeled, seeded and chopped
2 large tomatoes, chopped
1 - 2 jalapeno chile, stemmed, seeded
1 small red onion
salt
2 avocados, peeled, seeded and sliced
2 limes, cut into wedges

Directions

1. Place a heavy large saucepan over medium-high heat. Heat in it 1 inch of oil.
2. Cook in it the tortillas in batches until they become crunchy and golden.
3. Drain them and transfer them to paper towels.
4. Get a mixing bowl: Stir in it the shrimp, crab, lemon juice, cilantro, cucumbers, tomatoes, jalapenos, onions, and salt.
5. Arrange your tortilla crackers on a serving plate. Spoon over them the ceviche then serve them.
6. Enjoy.

Ceviche Tilapia

Prep Time: 30 mins
Total Time: 30 mins

Servings per Recipe: 6
Calories   188.8
Fat   2.8g
Cholesterol   75.6mg
Sodium   470.2mg
Carbohydrates   13.2g
Protein   31.6g

Ingredients

- 2 lbs. tilapia fillets, cubed
- 8 -10 garlic cloves, chopped
- 1 tsp salt
- 1/2 tsp black pepper
- 2 tsp fresh cilantro, chopped
- 1 habanero pepper, seeded and chopped
- 8 -12 limes, squeezed and strained to remove pulp
- 1 red onion, sliced and rinsed

Directions

1. Get a large mixing bowl: Stir in it fish fillets with garlic, cilantro, pepper, lime juice, salt, and pepper.
2. Lay the onion slices on top. Place it in the fridge for 3 h.
3. Once the time is up, serve your ceviche with some lettuce, corn, and avocado.
4. Enjoy.

CEVICHE Bowls

Prep Time: 10 mins
Total Time: 10 mins

Servings per Recipe: 4
Calories	365.6
Fat	14.7g
Cholesterol	53.8mg
Sodium	83.3mg
Carbohydrates	24.7g
Protein	35.5g

Ingredients

- 20 oz. ahi tuna, cubed
- 1 fresh mango, peeled and cubed
- 1 fresh avocado, peeled and cubed
- 2 tbsp red onions, minced
- 1 tomatoes, roasted, peeled & seeded
- 1 serrano pepper, roasted, seeded & minced
- 1/2 C. lime juice
- 1/2 C. orange juice
- 1/8 C. tomato juice
- 1 dash Tabasco sauce
- 1 pinch sugar
- salt

Directions

1. Get a mixing bowl: Stir in it half of the lime, orange and tomato juice with tuna cubes.
2. Stir in the red onions, with roasted tomatoes, pepper, Tabasco sauce, sugar, and salt.
3. Place it in the fridge for at least 4 h.
4. Once the time is up, drain it and place it aside.
5. Stir them with the half of strained juices. Repeat the process with avocado.
6. Place small size mold in each plate. Press in it the mango, followed by avocado and fish mixture.
7. Pat them down and place them in the fridge for at least 2 h.
8. Once the time is up, gently remove your molds then serve your ceviche right away.
9. Enjoy.

Sonoma Fruit Salad

Prep Time: 20 mins
Total Time: 20 mins

Servings per Recipe: 4
Calories   468.8
Fat   26.3g
Cholesterol   0.0mg
Sodium   214.5mg
Carbohydrates   62.3g
Protein   4.2g

Ingredients

Salad
1 green apple, cored and chopped
1 ripe avocado, peeled, pitted and chopped
1 banana, peeled and chopped
1 (11 oz.) cans mandarin oranges, drained
1/4 C. raisins
1/4 C. nuts, chopped
Dressing
1 tsp lemon juice
1/4 C. orange juice
1/4 C. canola oil
1/3 C. honey
1/4 tsp Dijon mustard
1/4 tsp salt
1 1/2 tsp poppy seeds

Directions

1. For the salad: in a bowl, add all the ingredients and mix well.
2. For the dressing: in another bowl, add all the ingredients and beat until well combined.
3. Place the dressing over salad and gently, stir to combine.
4. Enjoy.

GROUND TURKEY
Tacos

🥣 Prep Time: 10 mins
⏲ Total Time: 20 mins

Servings per Recipe: 8
Calories 549 kcal
Carbohydrates 39.1 g
Cholesterol 84 mg
Fat 33.8 g
Protein 26.7 g
Sodium 872 mg

Ingredients

Tacos:
1 tbsp vegetable oil
1 pound lean (at least 93%) ground turkey
1 (1 oz.) package taco seasoning mix
2/3 cup water
1 (4.6 oz.) package taco shells
Toppings:

2 medium avocados, pitted, peeled and sliced
1 cup sliced pineapple (fresh or canned)

Directions

1. Cook turkey in hot oil over medium heat in a large skillet until you see that it is no longer pink.
2. Drain any water and add taco seasoning mix and some water before turning the heat down and cooking it for another 10 minutes or until you find that the sauce is getting thick.
3. Put this into taco shells.
4. Serve.

Avocado & Tomato Dip

Prep Time: 10 mins
Total Time: 10 mins

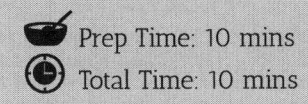

Servings per Recipe: 4
Calories   262 kcal
Fat   22.2 g
Carbohydrates   18g
Protein   3.7 g
Cholesterol   0 mg
Sodium   596 mg

Ingredients

- 3 avocados, peeled, pitted, and mashed
- 1 lime, juiced
- 1 tsp salt
- 1/2 C. diced onion
- 3 tbsps chopped fresh cilantro
- 2 roma tomatoes, diced
- 1 tsp minced garlic
- 1 pinch ground cayenne pepper

Directions

1. In a large bowl, mix together all the ingredients.
2. Serve immediately or you can refrigerate, covered for at least 1 hour for better flavor.

ENJOY THE RECIPES?

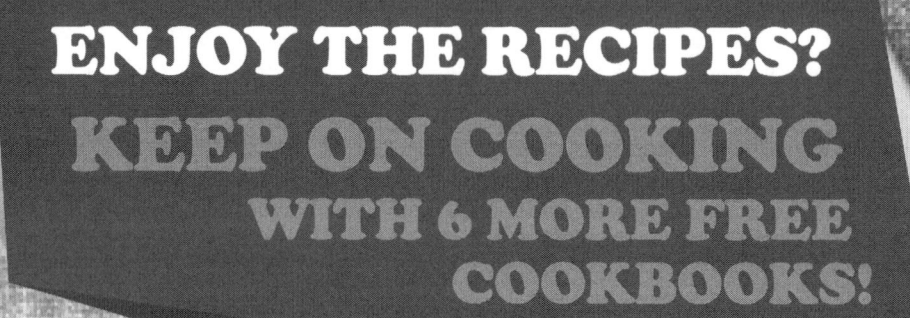

KEEP ON COOKING WITH 6 MORE FREE COOKBOOKS!

Visit our website and simply enter your email address to join the club and receive your 6 cookbooks.

http://booksumo.com/magnet

https://www.instagram.com/booksumopress/

https://www.facebook.com/booksumo/

Printed in Great Britain
by Amazon